Praise for
Is There an Engineer Inside You?

"This book is an excellent resource for a high school career counselor or any student interested in becoming an engineer."
—**The Science Teacher**

"A practical manual exploring the realities of work and career potentials."
—**Midwest Book Review**

"The book provides insights on how to think about an engineering education, get mentally conditioned, and succeed above your classmates."
—**Today's Librarian**

"Useful resource for would-be engineers and engineering students."
—**The Advising Quarterly**

"Book helps students find the engineer within."
—**Engineering Times**

"Students exploring the possibility of an engineering career will find guidance."
—**American Society for Engineering Education, Prism Magazine**

"Features no-nonsense smarts about studying engineering."
—**The NextSTEP Magazine**

"This is a 'must have' book for anyone considering an engineering career."
—**Satisfied Customer**

"Baine provides a realistic look at the skills and training necessary to succeed in engineering and at the great variety of jobs within the field."
—**Parent Press Magazine**

"The book features why getting an engineering degree may be the best thing a person could do for herself."
—**Tech Directions: Linking Education to Careers**

Is There an
Engineer
Inside You?

A Comprehensive Guide to Career Decisions in Engineering

Celeste Baine

Fourth Edition

Engineering Education
Service Center
Eugene, OR

Is There an Engineer Inside You?
A Comprehensive Guide to Career Decisions in Engineering (Fourth Edition)

by Celeste Baine

Published by:
Engineering Education Service Center (imprint of Bonamy Publishing)
1004 5th Street
Springfield, OR 97477 U.S.A.
(541) 988-1005
www.engineeringedu.com

Copyright © 2015, 2014, 2013, 2012, 2002, 1998 by Celeste Baine

Printed in the United States of America

Publishers Cataloging-in-Publication
Baine, Celeste
     Is there an engineer inside you? a comprehensive guide to career decisions in engineering. Fourth Edition.
     p. cm
     Library of Congress Control Number: 2001119308
Includes bibliographical references and index.
     ISBN 978-0-9819300-7-7 (pbk.)
     1. engineering—vocational guidance. 2. career education—handbooks, manuals, etc. 3. engineering—study and teaching "HIGHER". I. Title. II. Baine, Celeste.

How to Order:
Single copies may be ordered from the Engineering Education Service Center, 1004 5th Street, Springfield, OR 97477; telephone (541) 988-1005. www.engineeringedu.com. Quantity discounts are also available.

*this book is dedicated to
that spark of genius in all of us*

Other Engineering Career Publications by Celeste Baine

The Green Engineer: Engineering Careers to Save the Earth. $19.95

The Maritime Engineer: Careers in Naval Architecture and Marine, Ocean and Naval Engineering. $17.95

The Musical Engineer: A Music Enthusiast's Guide to Engineering and Technology Careers. $17.95

The Fantastical Engineer: A Thrillseeker's Guide to Careers in Theme Park Engineering. $17.95

High Tech Hot Shots: Careers in Sports Engineering. $19.95

Ideas in Action: A Girl's Guide to Careers in Engineering $7.95

Careers in Robotics - Coming Soon!

www.engineeringedu.com

Acknowledgments

My thanks and gratitude go to the many professors, engineers, counselors, students, and recent graduates for the information and contributions they have made to this work. I cannot list every source consulted in the preparation of this manual; the list is too extensive.

Several engineering societies have given information generously and contributed to this manuscript. I especially want to thank the following organizations and writers for their contributions: The American Institute of Chemical Engineers: Food for Thought – The Engineer Who Came to Dinner; Ed Sobey, President of the Northwest Invention Center: Invent it Today! ; American Society of Mechanical Engineers: George Washington – The First U.S. Engineer.; Bob Ratliff, Mississippi State University: Aerospace grad making his mark on the game of golf — and on the golf ball.; American Society of Agricultural and Biological Engineers: Oceans of Opportunity.; The Ceramic Engineering Department at the Missouri University of Science and Technology: Tasks of Ceramic Engineers.; Ivar Sanders: The Footsteps of an Electrical Engineer.; Charles Wright: The Footsteps of an Environmental Engineer.; American Society of Heating, Refrigerating and Air-Conditioning Engineers: Refrigeration, Milton Garland: One "Cool" Engineer.; Maribeth McCarthy: The Footsteps of a Metallurgical Engineer.

Many thanks also to the ASEE's Engineering Technology listserve for helping to ensure the accuracy of the engineering technology content. For your generous contribution, my gratitude goes to: Dr. Adrienne Y. Smith, Dean, Engineering Technology, Springfield Technical Community; Brian Bennett, Assistant Professor, University of Alaska Anchorage; Brian Norton, Assistance Professor, Oklahoma State University; Cheryl Simmers, Assistant Director, Appomattox Regional Governor's School for the Arts and Technology; Christine Halsey, Professor, DeVry University; Dr. Daniel Wong, College of the North Atlantic; Daphene Koch, PhD, Associate Professor, College of Technology, Purdue University; David Meredith, Associate Professor of Engineering, Penn State Fayette; Prof. Dennis E. Kroll, Ph.D. Bradley University; Dr. Doug Hicks, Department Chair for Engineering Technologies, Delaware Technical Community College; E. Daniel Kirby, Assistant Professor, Central Connecticut State University; Edward R. Evans, Jr. PE, Department Chair and Senior Lecturer, Mechanical Engineering Technology, Penn State Erie, The Behrend College; Dr. Elke Howe, Department Head Engineering Technology, Missouri Southern State University; Eric K. McKell, PE, Brigham Young University; Florian Misoc, Ph.D., PE., Associate Professor,

Southern Polytechnic State University; Frank A. Gourley Jr.; Gerald K. Herder, Cal Poly Pomona; Gerry Hieronymus, PT instructor, Central Piedmont Community College; I.J. LeBlond; Iskandar Hack, Associate Professor and Chair, MCET Department, Indiana-Purdue at Fort Wayne; Jacqueline H. Smith, Assistant Professor, Chattanooga State Community College; John B. Nicholas, PhD Assistant Professor of CIS, The University of Akron; Jonathan Fischer, Assistant Professor, Dept of Engineering Technology, California Maritime Academy; Kathleen L. Kitto, Western Washington University, Acting Dean of the Graduate School and Vice Provost for Research, Special Assistant to the Provost for Strategic Initiatives; Kathy Tarnai-Lokhorst, P.Eng, MBA, Instructor, Camosun College; Kristen Dagan McGee, Associate Professor/Electronic Engineering Technology Coordinator, Naugatuck Valley Community College; Lawrence H. Beaty, Idaho State University, Executive Director and Chair, Energy Systems Technology and Education Center; Louis Gennaro, Professor Emeritus, Rochester Institute of Technology; Dr. Marilyn Barger, PE; Martha Garcia-Saenz, Associate Professor & Program Coordinator of Construction Engineering & Management Technology at Purdue University North Central; Mel Whiteside, Director, Engineering Technology, Wichita State University; Michael Fisch, Associate Professor, Kent State University; Mike Pitcher; Mostafa A. Tossi, P.E., Senior Instructor of Engineering, Penn State University; Mulchand Rathod, Professor, Wayne State University; Edward Z. Moore, Assistant Professor, Central Connecticut State University; Paige Wyatt, Department Lead Engineering Technology, Columbia Basin College; Dr. Ralph Sprang, Lecturer, Penn State Erie, the Behrend College; Professor Randy Winzer, Pittsburg State University; Ray Floyd, Adjunct Professor, Northwest College; Richard Hemingway, Assistant Professor, Salt Lake Community College; Palmerino Mazzucco, Faculty, Mesa Community College; Sathya Gangadharan, Embry Riddle Aeronautical University; Scott A. Sabol, Professor, Vermont Technical College; Stanley Klemetson, Ph.D., P.E., Associate Dean of College of Technology & Computing, Utah Valley University; Terrence P. O'Connor; Thomas Laverghetta, Indiana Purdue University; Tom McGovern, Associate Professor, St Louis Community College; Timothy W Zeigler, Chair, Civil Engineering Technology Department, Southern Polytechnic State University; Tom Lombardo, Ed.D., Professor, Rock Valley College; and Wayne A. Whitfield, Ph.D., Associate Professor, Industrial Technology Dept., Fitchburg State University.

Contents

Preface

Part I, What is Engineering?

Chapter 1

Surf's Up in Engineering 17
It's Not All About Math 20
What Do They Do? 22
Engineers are Creative? 23
What Does an Engineer Look Like? 25
Why Chooses Engineering 25
Your Success Depends on You 27
    SUMMER CAMPS 29
    STUDENT COMPETITIONS/CONTESTS 30
    ENGINEERING PROJECTS IN COMMUNIY SERVICE 31
Match Your Personality 32
Assess Yourself 33

Chapter 2

Choosing Engineering or Engineering Technology 35
    ENGINEERING TECHNOLOGIST & TECHNICIAN FUNCTIONS...37
    ENGINEERS 38
    ENGINEERING TECHNOLOGISTS 39
    ENGINEERING TECHNICIANS 42
What is a Professional Engineer? 45
    ENGINEERING INTERN 45

Chapter 3

Gearing Up for College 47
    COMMUNITY COLLEGE PROGRAMS 48
    FOUR YEAR COLLEGES AND UNIVERSITIES 50
    ARTICULATION AGREEMENTS 51
    ENGINEERING CURRICULA 52

MANAGE YOUR TIME..52
STUDY SMART...52
FIND A MENTOR..53
Choosing the Right School **54**
ACCELERATED PROGRAMS...56
CO-OPS AND INTERNSHIPS...57

Chapter 4

Women in Engineering 59

Chapter 5

Minorities in Engineering 65

Chapter 6

"Wow!" Careers in Engineering 69
Peace Corps 69
Engineers Without Borders 70
Imagineering 71
Sports Equipment Design 73
Music Engineering 74
Green Energy Engineering 75
Space Engineering 76
Engineering for Animal Health 77
Engineering in Business...78
Inventing Products 79
   Feature Article - Invent it Today!
Engineers in Politics..81
   Feature Article - George Washington - The First U.S. Engineer
The Bachelor of Art in Engineering 84

Part II, The Many Faces of Engineering

Salary Information 85
AERONAUTICAL / AEROSPACE ENGINEERING 87
    Feature Article - Aerospace grad making his mark on the
    game of golf -- and on the golf ball
AGRICULTURAL AND BIOLOGICAL ENGINEERING 92
    Feature Article - Oceans of Opportunity
ARCHITECTURAL ENGINEERING 96
AUTOMOTIVE ENGINEERING 97
BIOMEDICAL ENGINEERING 99
BIOMEDICAL ENGINEERING TECHNOLOGY 105
CERAMIC ENGINEERING 108
CHEMICAL ENGINEERING 110
CIVIL ENGINEERING 112
CIVIL OR CONSTRUCTION ENGINEERING TECHNOLOGY 116
COMPUTER ENGINEERING 119
COMPUTER ENGINEERING TECHNOLOGY 121
ELECTRICAL ENGINEERING 124
    The Footsteps of an Electrical Engineer
ELECTRONIC / ELECTRICAL ENGINEERING TECHNOLOGY 128
ENVIRONMENTAL ENGINEERING 131
    The Footsteps of an Environmental Engineer
FIRE PROTECTION ENGINEERING 135
FIRE PROTECTION ENGINEERING TECHNOLOGY 137
FOOD ENGINEERING 138
    Feature Article - Food for Thought - The Engineer Who Came
    to Dinner
HEATING, VENTILATING, REFRIGERATING, AND AIR-CONDITIONING ENGINEERING ... 141
    Feature Article - Refrigeration, Milton Garland: One "Cool"
    Engineer
INDUSTRIAL ENGINEERING 143
INDUSTRIAL ENGINEERING TECHNOLOGY 145
MANUFACTURING ENGINEERING 147
MANUFACTURING ENGINEERING TECHNOLOGY 148
MARINE ENGINEERING 152
MARINE ENGINEERING TECHNOLOGY 156
MATERIALS ENGINEERING 158
    Feature Article - Smart Engineering
MECHANICAL ENGINEERING 164

MECHANICAL ENGINEERING TECHNOLOGY 166
METALLURGICAL ENGINEERING 169
   The Footsteps of a Metallurgical Engineer
NAVAL ARCHITECTURE 172
OCEAN ENGINEERING 174
OPTICAL ENGINEERING 175
PETROLEUM ENGINEERING 176
PHARMACEUTICAL ENGINEERING 177
PLASTICS ENGINEERING 179
ROBOTIC ENGINEERING 180
SOFTWARE ENGINEERING 183
STRUCTURAL ENGINEERING 185
SYSTEMS ENGINEERING 186
TELECOMMUNICATIONS ENGINEERING 188
TRANSPORTATION ENGINEERING 189

Appendix

50 Reasons to Become an Engineer 191

ABET Accredited Programs in Engineering..........................193

ABET Accredited Programs in Engineering Technology...194

Bibliography/ Recommended Reading 195

Preface

When you tell your parents you want to study engineering, they naturally beam with pride. Your friends and acquaintances suddenly put you in a different intellectual bracket than before. People you've just met start asking you questions about math or ask you to fix their computer. Everyone wishes you good luck as you leave for the first day of class.

When I decided to go to engineering school, I packed up everything I owned and headed east to Louisiana. I wanted to study biomedical engineering and at that time, there weren't too many affordable programs around. I looked up a list of the top ten programs and chose the smallest college. I wanted small class sizes and a very personalized experience. I wanted to make an impact on my professors, university and community. I had big dreams and I hoped my professors would remember me years later.

I was a very serious student and worried about making A's in everything my first year. I thought my future employers needed a straight-A graduate. In my second calculus class, my ideal world began to slip away. All students have at least one class with a professor they don't like or can't understand. This was my class. I had finally met a professor I thought I couldn't learn from. His math instruction seemed to just bounce off of my skull – I didn't get it. He would lecture and tell jokes, but I couldn't laugh; his jokes weren't funny because I couldn't understand what he was trying to say. I would go home, struggle, and sometimes cry when I tried to do the work he assigned. Every day I forced myself to open my notes and try again. Most days, I felt as if I was pounding my head against the wall. I began to think that maybe I was in the wrong major. Maybe engineering was for the elite. Maybe I didn't fit the model of what engineering students were supposed to be. This must be why everyone complained about the difficulties associated with obtaining an engineering education.

Thankfully, that class ended, and I continued to pursue my education. And it turned out that the experience I gained from

13

learning to deal with that difficult professor came in handy over the next two years. It is impossible to avoid professors you don't like or who are not good teachers. But you can learn the essential strategy that will get you through school: taking responsibility for your own learning and becoming excellent at taking tests. Try to see your professors from a different angle by visiting them in their office or e-mailing a question to them related to their class. Sometimes an office visit can remind you that they are real people and not someone your imagination dreamed up to torture you. Fortunately, most professors genuinely want you to succeed.

When I started engineering school, I had never used a power tool or designed anything in a Computer Aided Design (CAD) system. By my second year of engineering school, I felt frustrated because it seemed like all of my male friends could understand the concepts more easily — I thought they had been born with some intuitive understanding about engineering. After a particularly difficult calculus test, I went to my adviser to whine, grovel and basically complain about my inability to "get it." In the midst of my rant about all that was wrong with the system, he said, "Celeste, forget about that, the world needs all kinds of engineers." I sat there wondering why I hadn't realized that earlier. I might not get it the fastest — or be a math superstar — but there was a destination out there for me, a destination that fit my personality and one I would enjoy.

Finding a good fit is so important - that's why this book is written from the perspective of an engineering student, not an educator. Students, rather than educators, know what is interesting to other students and know what you need to know to get through an engineering program. This book doesn't focus on how a class is taught but on how to prepare for college and how to find the resources available to ensure that you succeed. An engineering education can open the door to a new world of possibilities you never suspected existed. When you finish your degree and you are an engineer, you will have the confidence and know-how to become anything you want to be.

This book developed out of my desire to extinguish the myths and stereotypes of engineers. In part, my rejection of those false beliefs comes from the fact that I'm a minority and a woman in a male-dominated field. I am an engineer, and I have many friends in engineering who don't fit the antiquated stereotypes: they are fun-loving people that have tremendous curiosity about the world and the people in it. Many became engineers because they wanted to make a difference in the lives of those they love. Improving medicine, being on the cutting edge of technology and creating a healthier planet were all reasons that I frequently heard for becoming an engineer. In fact, the more I learn about engineering, the more I've come to realize that engineers are some of the most creative and caring people on the planet. The most successful are well-rounded people who enjoy music, playing sports, and hanging out with friends.

It is true that with your education in engineering, an abundance of jobs will be open to you. It is true that if you make good grades, you can get almost any all-star job you want. But, do you need to take the traditional path and walk in the footsteps of the engineers before you? Are there alternative paths? What about women and minorities in engineering? What about the person who has other skills that can add new dimensions to traditional engineering? What about the person who studies engineering only as a launching pad for a different career – such as environmental engineers who become attorneys and biomedical engineers who become physicians?

This book will show you some of the most popular and most dramatic career opportunities I've uncovered in my quest for alternatives. If you were to ask me today, I'd tell you that even though I don't do engineering on a daily basis, becoming an engineer was among the best things I've ever done in my life. Studying engineering, although painful at times, is also one of the best gifts you can give to yourself. You will develop analytical and logical thinking skills that will help you in most everything you do for the rest of your life. An education in engineering will prepare you for life in a way that nothing else can.

Part I

What is Engineering?

Chapter 1

Surf's Up in Engineering

Think it, dream it and go for it! You want to make a difference, right? You've worked hard in school and you're ready to be part of the next big thing. An engineering education is a chance to explore, invent, and shape the world. It's a field that is endlessly creative, innovating and pioneering. Improving medicine, being on the cutting edge of technology and creating a healthier planet are all amazing reasons for becoming an engineer because engineers have the rare and incredible opportunity to make a difference in the lives of those they love. Within the field, there is much job satisfaction and an ability to point to a product and say, "I did that."

Engineering is also about designing a more humanistic future—one that considers people and a healthy planet as much as the bottom line. Engineers work hard to protect our scarce natural resources and care deeply about all of the creatures that inhabit our fragile world.

Don't forget that many of the jobs you may see in the next 10 years haven't even been invented. Many up and coming engineers will not only create new products but new engineering sectors as well. Biomimicry (problem-solving inspired by nature) alone offers numerous possibilities for building design, ventilation systems, electrical systems and many other things. Biomass opens up a whole host of possibilities for new fuels, paints, solvents, finishes, and other products to replace chemically produced products that are toxic. Sustainable solutions range from very simple things like using sustainably grown wood, encouraging landowners to grow trees, which capture and store carbon dioxide, to recently announced buildings that "breathe" by circulating fresh air. Get your degree, get some experience, and be ready. Engineers are leading the way to helping people by making the world a better place. The possibilities are endless for a motivated student.

A career in engineering is rarely boring! Today's engineering majors might find themselves at work on any of the following scenarios:

- A test engineer crashing expensive sports cars into walls to make them safer.
- A forensic engineer evaluating crime scene evidence to narrow down the search for a criminal.
- A design engineer creating a robot that can save people from burning buildings.
- A chemical engineer looking for ways to put solar cells into the paint of cars so that electric cars never need to be plugged in.
- A pharmaceutical engineer designing or synthesizing a cure for a disease that has affected millions.
- An architectural engineer designing green buildings that have the capability to power themselves.
- A biomedical engineer designing prosthetics that allow an artificial hand to feel.
- An electrical engineer specializing in solar and wind energy to provide electricity to an underdeveloped town or country, and so much more!

Engineering is one of the most progressive, challenging, and rewarding fields that can be studied today. Many people want to be engineers, have the ability and natural curiosity to succeed. Last year in the U.S. alone, 83,000 students graduated with engineering degrees. That graduation milestone required drive and perseverance. How do you get the drive and perseverance? Simply stated, you have to be willing to make the effort, take responsibility for your education, and not let anything stand in your way. You have to know what you are getting into and have a clear idea about what you want.

The word "engineer" literally means 'one who practices ingenuity'. There are droves of people who practice ingenuity – with or without a degree. But the degreed engineers will tell you that an engineering education teaches you how to think through any problem—and that is valuable to all professions. Individuals with a bachelor's degree in engineering enjoy some of the highest starting salaries of all baccalaureate graduates. Take a look at the job postings for just about any company and you'll find several ads for fabulous job opportunities for engineers. Engineering is the second largest profession in the nation with more than 2.3 million engineers in our nation's workforce. With more than 50 major branches of engineering and engineering technology and over 100 specialties, there is something for everyone who pursues a career in the field. Your personal goals, skills, and personality will determine which branch or specialty of engineering is right for you.

So, what is engineering? According to Jeff Lenard of the American Institute of Chemical Engineers (AIChE), the role of the engineer is perhaps one of the least understood in society. In any poll asking what engineers do, the responses invariably include "fix cars" and "drive trains." We see doctors, lawyers, and police on television, but where are the engineers?

Even though we don't see them, people have always held engineers in high regard; after all, engineers make the world go around. Engineering is all around us; as a career it may be the best way to make the biggest contribution to society. Engineers work to improve our health, happiness, and safety. They improve the quality of life and to make it more efficient or comfortable. They strive for constant improvement by applying scientific principles to solve everyday or specialized problems in practical ways. Engineers may design products such as smart phones or design systems such as the satellites, towers and routers that the phones need to connect anyone around the world.

A common misconception about studying engineering is that engineering is only for the intellectual elite or that it's only for students getting A's in math and science in high school. Engineering is a way to make life better. Many problems are solved by applying math principles, but math is just one tool in the engineer's toolbox. Inspiration, experimentation, vision, analytical ability, creativity, curiosity, imagination, energy, passion and communication skills are also extremely important.

There is no standard of intelligence needed to complete a degree in engineering. Excellent grades in math and science through high school, although nice to have, are not prerequisites to becoming a good engineer. Many students who have trouble in high school find out later when they try to work on a stimulating problem, they enjoy the problem-solving process and solutions come easily.

There is also no limit on the amount of time it takes to complete a degree. Whether a program of study takes 4, 5 or 6 years, the degree received and the job opportunities are the same. Some students delay graduation to participate in a co-op program, complete a minor, and/or take part in student activities. Others may have changed majors, held a part-time job, or took a light load to excel in their class-work. An engineering student who is willing to work hard and keep at it when things get tough, can expect a nice paycheck as well as a challenging and stimulating career. If you feel you have the aptitude and you make the commitment, you can and will succeed in engineering school.

It's Not all About Math

Suppose you are a B student in math and science, a good team leader and you excel at communicating. Traditionally, career advisors might have steered you away from engineering because you don't have an A in math and good communicators are needed in every profession. But if you have the drive and motivation to get through those math and science courses, you could become one of the most appreciated types of engineers; it's a highly valued skill to communicate the language of engineering to news media, the general public and within your own team – engineers don't work alone and are often in multi-national teams. According to George D. Peterson, former executive director of the Accreditation Board for Engineering and Technology (ABET),

"Employers claim that engineering success today requires more than up-to-the-minute technical capability; it requires the ability to communicate, work in teams, think creatively, learn quickly, and value diversity." There is a tremendous need for engineers who have excellent verbal and written skills. Scan the job descriptions of most engineering positions and you'll see what I mean.

Many people struggle with math – perceptions about math have changed the course of millions of lives. Sometimes, difficulty with math in elementary school was enough to change your direction, and sometimes it's about the challenge of many details — like changing a minus sign to plus when putting numbers on the other side of the equal sign. Sometimes, tending to the details of math (and life) can seem overwhelming.

The important thing is to learn why and when math should be applied, and to know what the approximate answer should be before entering an equation into a calculator or computer. For example, if an engineer enters an equation and the computer doesn't output an "expected" answer, that may tell the engineer an assumption or part of an equation might not be correct.

With that said, it's very important to take as much math as possible in high school. While you don't have to be a math wizard, it is important that you expose yourself to the math. Without at least four years of high school math, you will have to take extra time in college to take the necessary math courses. Math is very important for intellectual development including creativity, constructive processes and problem solving.

But math is just one tool in the engineer's box. Math and science are important tools to understanding the world and getting through most engineering classes, but they are not the only tools that an engineer uses to solve problems. Fortunately, in engineering there are thousands of different types of jobs. A student can choose a job that is very math intensive or a job that prioritizes different tools such as innovation, mechanical aptitude, or scientific knowledge in problem solving. Jobs in design usually require more math whereas jobs in training, sales and marketing require the least amount of math.

What Do They Do?

Engineers are modern day superheroes and as such, must be ready for anything in an increasingly technology-dependent world. Using math, science, knowledge, creativity, curiosity, and ingenuity in practical ways, they design, invent, create and concoct the most remarkable physical achievements and significant advancements in quality of life known to humanity. They are some of the most creative people on earth. Engineers make the stuff of our lives better, easier, more affordable, efficient and fun by solving everyday problems.

Think of them as practical inventors. Through the work of engineers, we are able to have iPhones, camera phones, wireless computers, HD video, satellite TV, airplanes, wind farms, electric cars, high-speed trains, digital music, underwater robots, air-conditioning, cosmetics, and titanium knee and hip replacements. The list goes on and on. Engineers have enabled us to explore the galaxy, break the sound barrier in a car, replace broken body parts, instantly connect with friends and family all over the world and so much more.

Almost everything you touch has been influenced or designed by an engineer directly or indirectly. It is impossible to think of a major technical development that hasn't included the work of engineers. Many internationally famous companies such as Intel, Google, Facebook, eBay, and Apple Computers wouldn't exist if one or more practical inventors (engineers!) hadn't gotten together and made them happen. Solidly rooted in engineering, these companies have grown into giants.

If you want to reduce pollution, end world hunger, become president of the United States (three presidents were engineers), improve the environment, invent exciting technology, become an astronaut, design race cars, solve complex problems, or make a world of difference, then engineering may be an excellent fit.

It is important to examine the shape and identify what kind of career you really want. Try to picture yourself in that role. Engineers and engineering technologists fall into two primary categories: one focuses on design engineering, and the other focuses on applications of engineering. For example, do you want to be on the engineering team that designs the next rover on Mars, or do you want to go to Mars with the rover? Do you want to be the engineer or engineering technologist who oversees production in an automobile factory, or do you want to be the expert engineer who gives presentations and answers technical questions on the new specialized suspension of that automobile? Do you want to design, build, maintain or fix the car? Innumerable doors open for engineering and engineering technology graduates, you just have to choose which door to go through.

Engineers are Creative?

Most people don't describe engineers as creative. Many people equate the word "creative" with being artists or writers. Engineers are just like artists except with a practical twist. They see a problem and apply creativity to find a solution. For example, millions of people all over the world dislike housework. The majority of people would rather be spending time with their friends or family instead of cleaning house. Engineers are the concept people and often the idea people too that have addressed and fixed or at least alleviated, with a little creativity, some of the more time consuming chores such as vacuuming.

Because consumers decided vacuuming was a problem, now we have the Roomba iRobot vacuum cleaner that automatically vacuums or mops floors while you do something more enjoyable. New homes often have vacuuming systems already installed in the walls or self-vacuuming kitchens, and Dyson engineers are always trying to design a better vacuum cleaner. In fact, a look at the advanced cleaning systems over the last 10 years further indicate just how frequently engineers are employed to find better cleaning solutions. Scrubbing Bubbles self-cleans your bathtub daily, the Swifter wants to mop your kitchen, and portable power-washers allow the average consumer to clean the exterior of their home and property without any other special equipment. Think about a world without dishwashing machines, microwave ovens, washing machines, dryers, refrigerators or freezers. Without engineers, so many day-to-day chores would be much harder.

On other technology fronts, engineers are the ones who figure out how to make a roller coaster careen forward at 120mph in four seconds without injury. They are the ones who figure out how to make cars run on electricity or fuel cell technology to keep our atmosphere cleaner. They also create medical equipment used by doctors to keep us healthy, and even work in the food industry to make foods such as chocolate and cereal taste better. Engineers have given us digital music, email and communications that fit into our pocket, and are hard at work to help save endangered animals from extinction and improve our environment.

Problem-solving has been the path by which some of the most amazing inventions and technologies have arrived in the market today. These inventions exist because one engineer had an idea. Look back at old pictures of the bicycle. People wanted the bicycle to go faster, to go up and down mountains and be more comfortable. The difference now is due to engineering. So that bikes could go off-road and through trails, engineers designed lightweight and stronger frames, along with shock absorbers, forks and wheels to take the punishment of off-road riding. When the cost of gas rose so much that more people wanted to ride bikes to work or school, engineers created a lightweight folding bicycle that could be carried into an office and unobtrusively stored or put into a school locker. When a faster bike was needed to win the Tour de France, engineers designed that too. Each year, engineers have gone back to the drawing board and made bicycles better. What will bicycles look like in another ten years? It's up to you and your imagination to tell us. You have the capacity to make the world a better place where people are safer, have more fun and can do more.

What Does an Engineer Look Like?

Engineering is slowly becoming more mainstream on TV and the Internet. The cable networks are showing more engineering, recycling/reusing and design programs and are starting to catch on to the appeal and significance of engineers' roles in society. As everyone becomes wiser to the work, engineers will be viewed for the pioneering problem-solvers they really are, lessening devastation from hurricanes, exploring other galaxies, and aiding in the cure of catastrophic illnesses. It will be a world in which people will say, "the engineer saved those people's lives" or "Thank you, engineer!"

There are currently 2.3 million engineers, engaged in everything from design to sales, including testing, manufacturing, training, and marketing. You can find engineers working in the field, behind a desk, in a production plant, at a customer site, or even on an airplane. Engineers design, manufacture, build, research, write, investigate and present their findings. It's easy to think of engineers designing rides at Disney or crawling around inside of a bridge to check for stress cracks but engineers also work invisibly behind the scenes. These engineers may be found checking air quality or researching new and safer ways to dispose of hazardous materials. They may be trying to find ways to save animals on the brink of extinction or working on developing safer foods, advanced farming techniques or ways to cut down on crime.

Why Choose Engineering

Engineering school can require a tremendous amount of time and effort; but, as technology continues to develop, the need for engineers, and the reward of being an engineer, will increase too. Some of the most popular reasons to be become an engineer include:

- Personal happiness: A primary reason people choose to study engineering is personal happiness. On the average, people spend 8 hours a day, 40 hours a week, 50 weeks a year at work. With only 24 hours in a day, the largest amount of time will be spent working, getting to work, and talking or thinking about work. Studies show that the leading cause of unhappiness in the United States is job dissatisfaction. With this in mind, why not beat the odds by finding a career that will keep you happy by providing great financial security, diversity, flexibility, prestige, intellectual development, challenges, and personal satisfaction? Happiness and pride in engineering come because most of the projects arise from an idea. Things start from scratch and end as an icon building, an impressive bridge, a robot that performs many task, a car that perform better than others, or medical equipment that saves lives. The variety of ideas and finished projects keep the engineer's job interesting.

- To work with other smart people and travel: People who enjoy working with other people and traveling may become sales or field service engineers. People who enjoy life's big picture may become the systems engineers who put all the pieces together. Creative people or people who constantly have new ideas about everything may enjoy working as design engineers. People who enjoy conducting experiments or working in laboratories may enjoy working as test engineers. In every scenario, engineers work with other smart people to solve problems locally or at the customer's location.

- To become a doctor or attorney: According to the American Medical Association, students with bachelor's degrees in biomedical engineering have a higher acceptance rate into medical school than students with any other undergraduate degree. If you want to become an attorney specializing in environmental law, a good way to start would be with an undergraduate degree in environmental engineering; a mechanical engineering degree would be a good foundation for someone who wants to become a patent attorney.

- To become an entrepreneur: Engineering also lends itself nicely to entrepreneurial types. In fact, more engineers are CEO's of companies than any other undergraduate degree. Usually this is because they invent something and then form a company to market and sell it. Other engineers may form construction, environmental, or consulting firms because their knowledge is in high demand. Some become inventors, and some become teachers or writers. Three engineering students even went on to become president of the United States (George Washington, Herbert Hoover and Jimmy Carter)!

- To lead engineering companies: Many engineers obtain higher degrees in business to become better managers and to receive a broader understanding of the inner workings of engineering companies. Many graduates work for financial companies; they may write software programs or construct financial models to predict Wall Street activities.

- To learn how to think: One of the best reasons to choose engineering is because an engineering education teaches you how to think through a problem in order to solve it. These mental agility skills will help you solve problems for the rest of your life. The fascinating aspect about problem solving in engineering is that there is almost never a "right" answer. You access several different approaches to solve a problem, and then it is up to you to show everyone how your solution meets the needs of the design.

- To make a difference and help people: Engineering is one of the most humanistic fields around. Engineering is about making life better.

Your Success Depends on You

Remember that this book is only one source of information to help you decide whether you want to become an engineer. Right now, you need to begin reading everything you can find about engineering and talk to every engineer or engineering student you know about the challenges ahead and how to prepare for them. Attend a summer camp or program pertaining to engineering at your school or nearby community college or university. You can never begin preparing for this career too soon. The more you expose yourself to the world of engineering, the more opportunities you may have and the better prepared you will be to meet the challenges ahead.

An often overlooked yet extremely valuable tool is communication skills. If you have ever played a team sport, you understand that teamwork is integral to the success of the team. Each player brings different strengths to the team, without which the team can't function as efficiently. Engineering design works in the same way. Each member of the team contributes, according to individual strengths, and the resultant learning and/or design produces a superior product. Jennifer Ocif, a performance footwear engineer at Reebok says, "Communication is a life skill that constantly needs attention and improvement. Unfortunately, it is not specifically taught in engineering classes but you can learn it by doing it anywhere. You just have to work at it because no matter how smart you are, if you can't communicate with the people you work with, your ideas will never go anywhere." People learn from each other, empower each other, and share the responsibility of finishing projects on time and on budget. Knowledgeable, effective teams can create extraordinary results by tapping into the strengths of each team member.

Engineers must also be able to communicate well with a wide variety of people. Each team member brings a different set of skills to the table. It's important to realize that different ideas and ways of thinking are exactly what can make a product, attraction, or company great. A diverse group of people working together usually equates to more detail and a better design or end result.

Get involved in extracurricular activities that involve math or science such as joining a robotics team. Part-time or summer jobs in engineering or manufacturing companies also show college admission departments you are serious about a career in engineering. There are numerous science and engineering camps available to motivated students.

Academic preparation is also essential to exploring engineering as a career. In high school, classes in algebra I and II, trigonometry, biology, physics, calculus, chemistry, computer programming, computer applications or engineering can tell you if you are academically prepared to study engineering. All of the above courses are not required to get into every engineering school, but early preparation can mean the difference between spending four years in college or six. Most colleges also require two to three years in a foreign language for admission. Check into the programs that interest you and begin to fulfill their requirements. Advanced Placement or Honors courses and an ACT score of 20 or SAT of 1000 are recommended.

SUMMER CAMPS

Summer camps provide another innovative approach to preparing for a career in engineering or evaluating if that career is right for you. Find out what it is like to study engineering, about the different types of engineers and what engineers do on a daily basis. Many universities across the country offer residential and local summer engineering camps for middle and high school students; the camps become more popular every year. They can help students develop leadership and professional and personal organizational skills; and they provide opportunities to meet and talk with engineers during visits to local engineering companies.

Nancy Fleming, an engineer, said she had the chance to learn about engineering in high school through an engineering camp at Wichita State University. Although she often struggled with math, when she decided to go to engineering school she says, "I can remember sitting in classes thinking I've got to be the dumbest person here, then I started getting good grades in those classes. I had to change my perception."

Engineering camp is a highly recommended introduction to the profession. These summer camps, usually hosted by engineering schools around the country, and may include engineering applications such as guitar making, creating sports equipment, designing alternative energy gadgets, building gliders, airplanes and rockets and writing video games. Check with the college of engineering or engineering technology at a university near you or for a directory of engineering camps, visit, engineeringedu.com.

STUDENT COMPETITIONS/CONTESTS
Another great way to get a feel for engineering is to look at the student design competitions that are sponsored or co-sponsored by various engineering societies and organizations. These competitions are developed to encourage and motivate students. The competitions focus on teamwork and allow the students to get a "real-world" feeling of the design process, cost of materials, and team dynamics/environment.

A few of the more popular competitions include:
- Intel International Science and Engineering Fair (ISEF). The ISEF, a program of Society for Science & the Public, is the world's largest pre-college science fair competition. www.societyforscience.org
- Boosting Engineering, Science, and Technology (BEST). A robotic competition that provides students with an intense, hands-on, real engineering and problem-solving experience that is also fun. www.bestinc.org
- FIRST Robotics Competition. Corporations and universities team up with high schools in a high-tech robot sporting event. www.usfirst.org
- Mathcounts. A national math coaching and competition program for 7th and 8th grade students. www.mathcounts.org
- Future City. Students learn about math and science in a challenging and interesting way through reality-based education. futurecity.org
- International Bridge Building Contest. The construction and testing of model bridges helps high school students develop "hands on" skills through bridge construction. By participating in the Bridge Building Competition students

get a flavor of what it is to be an engineer by designing structures to a set of specifications and then seeing them perform their function. bridgecontest.phys.iit.edu
- EESC Poster Contest. A graphic arts contest where students visually represent their understanding of engineering careers. www.engineeringedu.com

Competitions are also sponsored by the student chapters of engineering societies (i.e., ASME, ASCE, IEEE, SME). These competitions are often complex and are among teams of engineering students competing nationally against engineering students at other universities. The projects often require excellent communication and coordination within the teams and strict deadlines must be adhered to. The prizes range from trophies to cash and scholarships. For example, the American Society of Civil Engineers (ASCE) sponsors a "Concrete Canoe" competition for undergraduate students. The canoe must be made entirely out of concrete; it must float and even race against other concrete canoes created by students at other institutions.

ENGINEERING PROJECTS IN COMMUNITY SERVICE
If you are considering engineering as a way to change the world, you'll be happy to know about the Engineering Projects In Community Service (EPICS) program. EPICS encourages undergraduates to design, build, and deploy real systems to solve engineering-based problems for local community service and education organizations. Purdue University is headquarters for the National EPICS Program.

EPICS appeals to people who want to make a difference in their community. Currently, EPICS High includes 50 schools in 10 states and 23 international affiliate sites. More than 2,200 students participate. Of those, 44 percent are female and 61 percent are from minority groups.

Match Your Personality

It's important to choose a career that matches your personality. Find out as much about yourself as possible by taking personality assessments at career guidance centers and talking to friends, family, guidance counselors, and your math and science teachers. Check the want ads to see what employers expect and contact a local college of engineering or engineering technology to see if it offers tours or has programs for high school students.

Career placement and counseling centers usually offer the Myers-Briggs Type Indicator®, a primary assessment that may give you some insight into who you are, what conditions you may prefer to work under, and how you think about things. The test is designed to match your interests with the interests of people who are already in a particular occupation. Another resource is the Felder's Index of Learning Styles - available online for free. Some people are ideally suited to be "doers" in engineering. Doers are happy working on the front line of engineering companies designing, improving and/or maintaining systems and products. Some people, however, are better suited to applying their engineering background to research, sales, marketing, training, writing, and education – all fields in which they can contribute to society in beneficial ways.

The engineering personality can be anything:
- Extrovert or introvert;
- Someone who thrives on change, challenge, consistency or adversity;
- Engineers can be leaders or may prefer to let someone else lead;
- They will probably be hard working and lifetime learners;
- They may or may not be good under pressure and may or may not be effective communicators.

Friends and family may also provide excellent career advice. Typically, it is very difficult to be objective about your own personality. Friends might see strengths in your character that you never considered, or they may see weaknesses you hoped they wouldn't notice. Family members may see a "good fit" more easily than you can.

Consider the things you've done in the past. What have you enjoyed most? What have you found most frustrating or disliked most? If someone helped you solve that frustrating problem, would you still dislike it? Or would you feel as though you rose above the challenge? What does that tell you about yourself? Observe your friends, neighbors and relatives that are engineers and ask them if you can attend a day at work with them. There is a program called, "bring your child to work day" in many companies.

A word of caution: there is no "right" personality for a career in engineering just as there is no "right" type of engineer. If you have a genuine interest and desire to solve problems, and you are willing to put forth the effort to develop your skills and confidence in math and science, then science and engineering have something to offer you. The engineering profession needs all types of engineers and consists of all types of engineers.

Assess Yourself

Once you've decided that engineering is the right choice for you, take it a step further.

- Make a list of everything you like to do.
- Write down a description of your perfect job. Will you work inside or outside, at a desk or in a lab, etc.
- Write down your strengths and weaknesses.
- Think about why a certain job is a good fit for your personality or interests.

Because engineering is such a great way to combine your interests with your career, this is a way you can begin to determine your dream job. Once your assessment is complete, go to part two of this book and read through the career paths that are interesting to you. When you are reading, think about your answers to the questions above and see if you can integrate what you like to do in a job that allows you to utilize your strengths and interests. Once you find the paths that come close to your ideal, enroll in a summer camp or enter a competition that will allow you to explore the fields. Contact any local colleges that teach it and visit the department or go on a tour to learn more. This is your chance to explore if you will really like to go to college for engineering or engineering technology.

Chapter 2

Choosing Engineering or Engineering Technology

When the Soviet Union launched Sputnik in 1957, Americans took it as a threat to our technological superiority. Americans were afraid that they were falling behind the Soviet Union in science and engineering. This prompted universities to offer engineering coursework that was less applied (less laboratory time) and more theoretical. That left a gap between the designers (who could figure out anything that they could mathematically model) and the craftsman (who could build any device described by the designer.) Unfortunately, in this educational process, without the hands-on experience in college, the engineers could no longer communicate what they wanted built in the lab. For large corporations hiring engineers, this didn't cause a problem because they had the resources to train engineers on lab equipment. However, smaller companies that needed to hire engineers that could "hit the ground running" were between a rock and hard place.

The need for engineers that were more applications and practice oriented lead to the engineering technology (ET) degree. While some ET programs date from the 1940s, they really became popular in the 1960s. Engineering technology is offered as a bachelor's degree program (usually 4-5 years) and also as an associate's degree (usually 2-3 years) in varied fields of engineering. Graduates with a bachelor's degree in ET often get jobs with titles such as design engineer, manufacturing engineer, quality engineer, sales engineer, systems engineer, and plant engineer. Their responsibilities are similar to engineers and in most cases, at the bachelor's degree level, industry makes no distinction between engineers and engineering technologists – they are both hired as engineers.

However, not all companies feel the same. General Electric for example – will only hire ET graduates as engineers if they have the degree and a few years of experience. The differences between engineering and engineering technology jobs are related to the roles that engineers play in each company and industry. ET is not an inferior degree but reflects skills obtained for applying engineering within a company or industry. Whatever you choose, in all these programs it is important to realize that you will need to become a life-long learner so that your skills continue to grow and remain relevant.

In this text:
- An engineer is defined as a person with a bachelor's, or graduate degree in engineering
- An engineering technologist is defined as a person who has a bachelor's or graduate degree in any field of engineering technology
- An engineering technician is defined as a person who has an associate's degree or certificate of completion in any field of engineering technology

There are abundant job opportunities worldwide for engineers, engineering technologists and technicians who all use the principles and theories of science, engineering, and mathematics to solve technical problems. Engineers and engineering technologists are hired as engineers whereas engineering technicians are hired as technicians. The technician's work is usually more limited in scope and typically more hands-on than that of scientists and engineers.

Engineers usually build a "one of a kind" or the "first of a kind". The Space Shuttle was an engineering marvel and so was the first cell phone. But when cell phone manufacturers wanted to produce millions of phones a year, ET became much more important. In many design scenarios, the engineer develops the "big picture" and the ET graduate fleshes out the details.

Engineers are generally very focused on a very specific area. They are using theory to improve or develop products, technologies and systems. Technologists also design and develop products, technologies and systems but may also work alongside engineers in research and development applying their ideas to develop prototypes or test existing research. Others work in quality control, inspecting products and processes, conducting tests, or collecting data. In manufacturing, they may work in product design, development, quality control, test engineering, sales or production. They can be supervisors to connect the design professionals with the hourly workers. Every machine has a designer, a builder or fabricator, an installer, a maintainer, and someone who gets the machine ready to do what it is supposed to do. Engineers and technologists are usually the designers although the technologists may also build the machine, test it, support the design process led by an engineer, and get it ready to do what it is supposed to do. For example, technologists may develop the process settings so quality parts can be produced from that machine and the technicians usually install, maintain and program the machine. Another example would be that in the development of a new lamp, a designer has the idea on paper, the technologists applies the idea and oversees how other aspects of the lamp relate and the technician would review the practical applications of use and maintenance.

ENGINEERING TECHNOLOGIST & TECHNICIAN FUNCTIONS
Engineering technologists and technicians may find themselves planning, designing, testing, operating and analyzing machines, processes and installations. They may inspect operations and maintenance, install or operate components, or run tests on parts and equipment in a laboratory. They may also write reports, communicate with other members on the team and give presentations about their findings. A technologist that works in quality control could make sure that products are made to specification. A technologist in middle management could serve as the communication bridge between engineering and the facility.

In an industrial plant, a technician could remanufacture old equipment to bring it back to life. A technician or technologist with an interest in education could become a machine operations trainer, making sure that hospitals, companies, and individuals understand safe and effective procedures for using new equipment.

ENGINEERS

Engineers are trained to be very focused on one area such as electrical, mechanical, biomedical, chemical, etc. They want to understand why something occurs and like to have a theoretical understanding of a problem. An engineering education teaches the theoretical foundation of one specific area.

Engineers apply creativity, innovation, problem-solving, mathematics, and analytical thinking to whatever project or process they are designing or improving.

Advantages of an engineering degree include:

- Greater opportunity for advancement than an associate's degree
- Easier to continue to graduate school than engineering technology
- Ease of the professional licensure process compared to technology degree holders
- Great salary right out of school and excellent earning potential throughout your lifetime
- Education is very broad and provides the foundation to continue schooling to become doctors, lawyers, writers, teachers, and business people
- Understanding of high level math gives greater understanding of the world around you, and application of this to real problems can be very satisfying
- Consistently excellent job opportunities at the bachelor's degree level
- Engineers often escalate to management positions and earn more over the life of their careers

- Very rewarding to design products and/or processes that can save lives and benefit human-kind.

Disadvantages of an engineering degree include:

- The work can be stressful – especially when the work is associated with life and safety. For example, new medical devices are built to specification, on time, and on budget. If something goes wrong with the design and it threatens the life or safety of a person, the engineer's job (and peace of mind) may hang in the balance. She/he could lose their Professional Engineering license for life
- More time in school than an associate's degree (higher cost for college)
- Workload can be unpredictable and at times very high
- Competitive atmosphere for promotion (performance as perceived by superiors determines one's ability to be promoted)
- Fewer practical skills upon graduation. Often, engineering students have very little opportunity to take business, manufacturing, art, or writing courses
- Very rigorous and abstract mathematics is required - academic programs place a heavy emphasis on calculus, mathematics and analytical work

ENGINEERING TECHNOLOGISTS

The lines of separation between bachelor's level engineering and engineering technology positions in industry are blurring as the fields and responsibilities overlap more today than at any other time in history. Engineering Technology is a field that focuses on the application of established science, math, engineering and technology principles. A technologist is an expert at applying engineering principles and technology to solve problems and connect the theory to all aspects of the problem. An engineering technologist looks at the big picture and practical application of a problem. Both engineers and engineering technologists may design a product to solve a problem, but the engineer would be the one to discover new technology (like microwaves) or develop any new engineering principles and practices. The technologist would normally be the one to develop a product that uses the new technology (like a microwave oven) as well as adapting, building, installing and maintaining a new product or process. An engineer may design a product to solve a problem, but the technologist may develop the process to create that product quickly, inexpensively, and with high quality. Therefore, the technologist may be responsible for solving the problems that may occur in implementation.

With additional coursework, the technologist assists with the development and/or modification of a design in a broader aspect. The engineer has a very focused view of the product. Conversely, some engineers are also involved in the process design, but most of the time that is the work of a technologist.

Advantages of a bachelor's level engineering technology degree include:

- Consistently excellent job opportunities worldwide
- Some protection from out-sourcing to foreign countries because of their role in the building process of the machine or other product
- Less engineering theory and more applications-based education. Coursework may include real-world projects. You will be able to 'hit the ground running' in your career
- Work can be challenging and rewarding
- May be hired as an engineer and compete with students with engineering degrees for jobs
- Employers appreciate the real-world problem-solving aspects of your education
- Numerous areas of study available

Advantages of a bachelor's level engineering technology degree over an associate's degree include:

- Greater advancement opportunities than a technician
- Great salary right out of school and more earning potential throughout your lifetime

- Education of a technologist is very broad. Engineering technologists are able to take a wider variety of courses related to things like business, manufacturing, etc. depending on the discipline, since they have less math and science.
- Engineering technologists frequently climb high on the management career ladder
- More math and science requirements (to enable an easier transition to engineering, if desired)

Disadvantages of a bachelor's level engineering technology degree (compared to an associate's program) include:
- More time in school (higher cost for college)
- Can be challenging to move into engineering fields or degree programs, due to higher math requirements
- The work can be stressful
- May result in inability to become a licensed engineer in some states despite successfully performing engineering design work - not all states will allow this degree to be professional engineers
- Job opportunities may be limited because some larger companies have a policy to only hire four year engineering graduates
- May be performing similar work as an engineer but not receive comparable recognition and/or compensation

For the aspiring technologist, there are a variety of appropriate master's level degree programs. Earning a master's degree will open the doors to greater opportunities in management and technologies associated with technology. The degrees most-suitable to career advancement in an engineering enterprise are:
- Master of Business Administration
- Master of Technology Management
- Master of Science in any field of Engineering
- Master of Science in Engineering Technology
- Master of Science in Industrial Administration
- Master of Science in Computer Science

- Master of Science in Technology/Technical Education
- Master of Science in Industrial and/or Manufacturing Engineering
- PhD in Technology

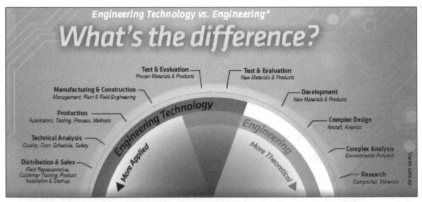

Program differences between bachelor of science programs in engineering technology and engineering. Reprinted with permission from the American Society of Mechanical Engineers (ASME) and Wichita State University.

Industry typically does not make disciplinary distinctions between engineering and engineering technology. The engineering technology disciplines virtually parallel their engineering counterparts. Those disciplines awarding the most bachelor's degrees, by rank, are: electrical and electronic, mechanical, industrial, construction, civil, manufacturing, computer, and general engineering technology. Other less common disciplines, by rank, are: architectural; aeronautical; chemical; drafting & design; nuclear; marine; electromechanical; automotive; mining/ metallurgy; and heating, ventilating, & air conditioning. See the appendix for a list of all of the engineering and engineering technology ABET accredited programs of study.

ENGINEERING TECHNICIANS

Engineering technicians with an associate's degree focus on applying established engineering technology principles in applications such as research and development, product design, manufacturing, and production processes. Engineering technicians work in research and development, build or set up equipment, prepare and conduct experiments, collect data, calculate or record results, conduct preliminary analysis and help engineers or scientists in other ways, such as making prototype versions of newly designed equipment. They also assist in design work, often using Computer-Aided Design (CAD) and/or Computer-Aided Design and Drafting (CADD) equipment. The engineering technician is concerned with applying technology to install and maintain machines and to aid in the interfaces between systems and people.

An engineering technician is defined as a person who has an associate's degree or certificate of completion in any field of engineering technology. Some technicians are trained within military schools and many are trained within non-credit programs that may not include any or little general education courses such as English or humanities.

Advantages of an associate's engineering technology degree include:
- Great salary for only two-three years of school
- Less time in school (this option also saves money)
- Abundant job opportunities worldwide and the jobs are not as vulnerable to outsourcing
- ET graduate is a preferred hire by many of the small local companies where the job duties tend to be more varied and growth potential can be huge
- The work is hands-on and often does not require the technician be stuck in an office or behind a desk
- Sometimes companies pay for you to complete your bachelor's degree
- Usually offered at nearby community colleges
- ABET accredited programs offer credits that are transferable to a Bachelor of Science engineering technology program. Sometimes this is difficult; see

disadvantages of transferring on page 48
- Practical and applied math and science – not as theoretical as engineering
- More classes in major – all technical courses you take are relevant and there are minimal general education requirements needed
- Since many fields have multiple technicians supporting one engineer the number of total jobs available is often greater for technicians than engineers
- Generally less stress, and you can leave work at work after quitting time

Disadvantages of an associate's engineering technology degree include:
- More competition for jobs
- It's difficult to transition from a technician to an engineer because most of the time, the science classes in an associate's level engineering technology program are not calculus based – therefore science classes must be repeated. Some community colleges have ways to get around this disadvantage such as "two for one" articulation agreements and bridge courses
- There is less long-term flexibility in the career and less opportunity for advancement unless you seek advanced training
- Salary increases may get smaller over time if you do not seek advanced education or training to stay current in your job skills
- The work can be stressful and demanding (but with less of the responsibility of an engineering technologist or engineer)

What is a Professional Engineer?

A professional engineer (PE) is one who has been licensed by a state to practice engineering (each state has similar, but different criteria for licensure.) Most engineers and engineering technologists are not licensed – licensure is not required for most practice of engineering. However, engineers who wish to be licensed must pass an eight-hour written exam called the Principles and Practices of Engineering to become a professional engineer. Many states restrict the title of engineer to those who have qualified through having successfully taken and passed both the Fundamentals of Engineering (FE) and Policies and Practices exams.

To become a PE, you must:
1. Graduate from an Engineering Accreditation Commission (EAC) / Accreditation Board for Engineering and Technology (ABET) accredited university program in engineering or engineering technology
2. Work four years (or seven years for engineering technology graduates) under the guidance of a professional engineer
3. Pass the FE and Policies and Practices exams.

ENGINEERING INTERN
Most states offer a pre-registration certificate called the Engineer Intern (EI) (formerly "Engineer in Training") to those right out of school who do not yet have four or seven years of experience. You can obtain the EI certificate by passing an eight-hour Fundamentals of Engineering (FE) test. An EI certificate is required to become a PE. A person is not eligible to sit for the Principles and Practice exam if they haven't passed the FE exam first.

The first half of the EI test challenges your general engineering skills. The last half pertains to a specific concentration in engineering such as chemical, civil, electrical, environmental, industrial, or mechanical. Although the certificate does not authorize the practice of engineering (you are not authorized to sign off on documents, projects, etc. that are released to the public) you can practice engineering as long as it is overseen and under the direction of a PE. It is the first step in the examination process for full registration. Then, after you gain four years of experience, you can take the PE examination. This test relates specifically to a major branch of engineering you studied and are practicing.

In most cases, engineers and technologists are licensed by a state and hold the liability and safety of the design. A technologist with a bachelor's degree, in most states, can take the Fundamentals of Engineering exam - the first step toward becoming a Professional Engineer (PE). However, this becoming less common. Some states are now baring ET bachelor's level graduates from becoming registered. The NCEES Model Law states that (as of January 1, 2020) "admission to an 8-hour written examination in the principles/practice of engineering will require that an engineer intern (EI) have -- (a) a master's degree in engineering from an institution that offers EAC/ABET accredited programs, or the equivalent, and with a specific record of 3 years or more of progressive experience." In addition, "the Model Law defines an engineer intern (EI) as a graduate of an engineering baccalaureate or masters program accredited by the EAC/ABET, or equivalent, who has passed the fundamentals of engineering (FE) exam."

For information pertaining to the rules and requirements about becoming a professional engineer, visit the National Society for Professional Engineers website under licensure and education: www.nspe.org or your own state's board for professional engineers.

Chapter 3

Gearing Up for College

"Education is the key to unlock the door to opportunities."
- George Washington Carver

Now that you have decided to pursue an engineering education, you should prepare for it as soon as possible. Search the Internet for information about colleges and universities and contact any engineering schools that are interesting. Browse their web pages. Ask about their programs and camps to help you prepare for college. Ask to talk to engineering students. Contact local engineering firms, and ask for a tour. Most firms would be happy to show you around and explain what they do. Several companies encourage continuous improvement in engineering education. For example, a company may have a summer intern program that allows college-level engineering students to work at their facility each year. Or, they may sponsor a job shadow program to bring junior high and high school students into the facilities or labs to see what their researchers are doing.

On the most basic level, college is designed to open doors. You will receive a well-rounded education as well as specific technical knowledge and skills. College teaches you how to think, solve ambiguous problems and use the tools of engineering such as design and simulation software – this gets you ready for employment.

There are several approaches to pursue an engineering or engineering technology career. You can attend a community or junior college, vocational school, technical college, state university or other public or private university. Programs range from one year or less for a certificate, two-three years for an associate's degree and four-five years for a bachelor's degree. Each path has its advantages and disadvantages. The important thing to remember is to take responsibility for your education and not let anything stand in the way of your goals. College classes are taught with the expectation that you are willing to do some research on your own and that you are motivated to do so. The coursework is very different from high school and much more rewarding.

COMMUNITY COLLEGE PROGRAMS

Community colleges are an asset to engineering and engineering technology programs. Engineering students often start their programs at community colleges by completing the lower division or pre-engineering programs offered by the school and then transfer to a university. Normally, enrollment in the courses is much smaller than comparable university courses, usually 15-30 versus 100+, providing more individualized instruction. Community colleges are accessible, affordable, and offer a very diverse mix of programs and services.

Additionally, many students get associate's degrees in engineering technology from community, technical or junior colleges. An advantage of an associate's engineering technology degree is that you can hit the ground running after graduation. Associate's programs typically provide practical coursework in the application of theory with an emphasis on the "hands-on" training as opposed to the bachelor's engineering programs that are dedicated to coursework in theoretical knowledge which develop skills and provide knowledge for more in-depth thinking which is required for research and design tasks. Employers are happy to hire technicians because their experience has given them the knowledge, hands-on skills, and ability to succeed in the workplace with relevant training.

If your high school grades don't allow you to get into the college or university of your choice, or you were not able to complete all of the math and science classes required for admission to a university program, spending two years or less at a community college completing your lower division classes can give you the chance to meet the requirements and get into the university of your choice. Community and technical colleges offer the ability to improve your math or writing skills in a less pressured environment. In addition, according to *Reverse Transfer: A National View of Student Mobility from Four-Year to Two-Year Institutions*, a study from the National

Student Clearinghouse Research Center, students who transfer from a community college tend to do better than those who started at a four-year school.

According to the AACC, the cornerstone of the community college mission is open access, which means that admission is open to anyone and everyone who seeks higher education. But don't take that too literally, most schools still have prerequisites, diploma, GED, and language skill entrance requirements. For some, community college is a transfer point to further education; for others, it is a final destination to employment or personal enrichment.

The **advantages** of attending community college are:

- Accessibility - Open enrollment means that students can enroll any time and begin classes at the start of any semester. Under-prepared students will find developmental courses to prepare them for college-level work. Be sure to check the admissions requirements of the community college to which you are applying to make sure you meet any deadlines they have set.
- Affordability - Many students take advantage of the lower cost to complete the first two years of course work toward a bachelor's degree before transferring. Tuition and fees are, on average, lower than those of universities.
- Career preparation - Students not intending to earn a degree will find programs and classes that provide the knowledge and skills in demand in a wide range of professional fields.
- Professors in community colleges are paid to teach, not perform research so more emphasis is placed on teaching.
- Class sizes are typically smaller at a community college, so there is more opportunity for students to interact directly with the professor.
- Numerous associate's degree programs in engineering technology are accredited by ABET.
- Many community colleges have articulation agreements in place that allow their graduates to transfer directly to university program with junior status (*see the section on articulation agreements on the next page*).

- A meaningful credential (AAS degree) after two years vs. nothing after two years in a bachelor's program.

The **disadvantages** of attending community college are:
- Transferring credits may not be a smooth process
- Arriving at a university in your junior year may be a difficult social transition. For example, it may be difficult to make friends with classmates who have already spent two years together.

FOUR YEAR COLLEGES AND UNIVERSITIES

Colleges and universities that offer bachelor's degrees in engineering and engineering technology are found all over the country. At these colleges, you can complete all four years of your bachelor's degree or transfer up to two years of credits from another college or junior college. Students who invest the time and money into a bachelor's degree will reap the benefits throughout their lives. Over the course of an entire career, the additional earning potential that comes with a bachelor's degree typically outweighs that additional initial cost. Colleges and universities offer students unique, well-rounded and flexible learning opportunities you simply can't find anywhere else.

As you consider colleges and universities for an engineering degree, note that many will require you to have calculus and physics on your high school transcript before they will accept you into their program. You should begin to review entrance requirements to determine if you need to take additional courses prior to applying or if there are alternative methods of admission (e.g., provisional, general education).

One difference between engineering and ET is that all engineering schools are ABET-accredited but fewer than half of the all ET schools have earned ABET accreditation. If you choose to pursue ET, it is very important to be sure your ET school has that credential. Industry set the content for what should be learned in each focused program and a team of industry practitioners and academic faculty visit the campus to verify that the school is really meeting the criteria.

ARTICULATION AGREEMENTS

Articulation agreements are contracts education programs make between each other guaranteeing that specific courses taken at one institution will be accepted for credit at another institution. This allows students to complete part of their bachelor's degree at a community college, and the remaining coursework at a university. Additionally, community colleges often work with their local and state universities and have articulation agreements to ensure their classes or most of the time, their entire associate's program (2+2 Program), will be accepted for transfer credit.

There are several types of articulation agreements. Check with your guidance counselor or the admissions office of your current institution as well as the admissions office of where you want to transfer for current and complete information.

- Transfer Admission Guarantee (TAG) Programs are designed to make transitioning from a community college to a 4-year university easier.
- 2+2 Programs ensure that an entire associate's degree program is transferable, with no loss in credits, to another institution.
- Some high school programs such as Project Lead the Way (PLTW) work with local colleges to align their curricula so students can take their high school level engineering courses for college credit.
- Advanced Placement (AP) courses also assure college credit to any student that is willing to work hard to pass the specific AP test.
- Early College high schools and other programs may offer dual enrollment courses that will provide college credit while students are still in high school.
- Some states offer technical education options that allow Career and Technical Education (CTE) classes such as electronics, machining, and CAD to be articulated into college credit.

ENGINEERING CURRICULA

Engineering curricula vary from school to school; however, most schools don't require you to declare a specific field of interest until the end of your second year. The first two years of engineering school are focused on learning the fundamentals such as chemistry, calculus, physics; and mechanics such as statics and dynamics. Courses in English, the humanities, and biology are usually required as well.

The third and fourth years of engineering school are most often spent studying your chosen specialty. Most universities require their students to complete a design project in their senior year. The project may be completed in teams or individually and solves a real-world problem. Students may be able to select a problem of personal interest, or local industry may present a problem they are currently exploring. Typically, the project requires a research report, and presentation of the design process and the results.

MANAGE YOUR TIME

Engineering is a rigorous and demanding major. To be successful in engineering school, you will need certain tools. You must be self-disciplined, willing to take responsibility for your education and also manage your time effectively. In college, the "real" learning often takes place outside the classroom, and less time is spent in the classroom. A general rule of thumb says that for every hour spent in the classroom, engineering students can expect to spend up to three hours outside the classroom, compared with two hours for non-technical majors. A good time-management system can also allow you to participate in extracurricular activities, which broaden your experience and are of interest to potential employers.

STUDY SMART

Alexander Astin, author of *What Matters in College: Four Critical Years Revisited*, says that the quality of a student's education is directly related to the student's "involvement." Astin says that successful engineering students need to devote an appropriate amount of time and effort to their studies. You need to:

- schedule your study time so that you master the material presented in each class session before the beginning of the next class session; share information frequently with peers and engage in group study and collaborative learning regularly
- interact frequently with professors in the classroom and in the professor's office
- spend as much time on campus as possible
- get involved in student organizations

You should also have a plan that you refer back to from time to time of what your future goals are and how what you are doing now relates to that. This helps to maintain your perspective when things get challenging.

By thinking about your study habits and preparing to change them now, you can make a big difference in the quality of your education. Free up your commitments when you begin school so you have fewer distractions. Be on the lookout for other people willing to study in groups. Visit your professors regularly. And join the local student chapter of the society for your engineering major. You will feel good about being at the top of your class.

FIND A MENTOR

Finding and developing a relationship with a mentor is a great idea. Mentors can help you figure out if engineering is the right career for you, they can alert you to opportunities such as job shadowing, summer jobs, engineering camps or other chances to learn about yourself. They can help you develop skills and deal with problems in school or at work.

There are many ways to find a mentor. Think about the people you can talk to about your career. Who will take a special interest in your goals? Who do you admire? Who do you want to model yourself after or emulate? Try to pick a mentor in your field of interest, but don't be limited by this approach. The most important thing is to find someone you respect, admire, and can talk to easily.

Some colleges and student engineering organizations have mentoring programs to support students. Ask your advisor or career counselor about available school programs or if they know of any upperclassmen who would be willing to help. A mentoring relationship demands considerable time, energy, trust, and a willingness to be open and honest about your goals and aspirations. If you are willing to put forth this effort, you may find that having a mentor can considerably aid you in meeting your goals and securing a fantastic career.

Choosing the Right School

Choosing the engineering or engineering technology school that is right for you is as important as wheels are to automobiles. Your choice will incorporate many of your preferences. Making the selection won't be easy. Hundreds of schools offer engineering programs; some schools have engineering dorms, some offer engineering fraternities or sororities, some are inner-city and some are spread out over large distances. The advantages and disadvantages of each school will depend on your personal needs and wants. Important considerations for most college-bound students include location, cost, faculty, school size, and academics.

- Location: In addition to distance from home, location refers to climate and the type of industry in the surrounding area. If there is industry specific to your degree, then opportunities for summer internships, co-op programs, and part-time work experience increase dramatically. These work experiences often lead to jobs after graduation.

- Cost: Cost of attendance may be a critical factor in determining which school to select, although your decision should not be based on cost alone. Generally, public institutions are less expensive than private schools, and in-state tuition is less than out-of-state tuition, but there are numerous ways to fund education at any institution. Most engineering societies offer scholarships (see a list of engineering societies at www. engineeringedu.com), and federal and state governments offer grants and loans. Part-time work, co-op programs, and campus jobs also help reduce the cost of attendance. Check with the financial aid department of the schools you are interested in to see what grants and loans you qualify for. Call the engineering department to find out about scholarships offered to incoming students through the college. The military may also offer opportunities for financing your education. The National Guard is a popular program among college students. The Air Force, Coast Guard, Marines, Merchant Marines, Army, and Navy offer education at reduced cost in exchange for a commitment to serve in the Armed Forces for a certain period of time.

- Faculty: A strong faculty makes it easier to get a good education. A diverse faculty will broaden your experience and better prepare you to work with people from many backgrounds. Faculty members can bring numerous experiences and expertise to their lectures. Check to make sure that faculty rather than graduate students teach the classes. As you proceed to junior-level and senior-level classes, the research of the faculty becomes more important. Try to select a school that has at least one faculty member performing active research or projects in your area of interest. That person can become a valuable role model and allow you to talk and learn directly from someone whose interests you share.

- School Size: School size matters for some students. Large schools offer a greater diversity of people and more things to do but often lack the professor-student interaction found at smaller schools. In a small school, you may get to know a larger percentage of classmates, but in a large school you can meet a much larger number of people. You can receive an excellent education at both large and small schools; which you choose is purely a matter of preference.

- Academics: Academics is probably the most important factor in choosing the school that's best for you. The program should be accredited by the Accreditation Board for Engineering and Technology (ABET). ABET accreditation ensures that the school program follows national standards for faculty, curricula, students, administration, facilities, and institutional commitment. By choosing an ABET program, you can be sure the faculty have met certain national standards and that the program is highly regarded by the profession.

Some students like the competitive atmosphere that accompanies attending a very prestigious school, and some students find they work better in a more relaxed environment. Both will require a great deal of studying, although some programs will be more challenging than others. Pick the atmosphere that best fits your personality and aspirations.

Some schools require their students to have computers; other schools provide computer laboratories. Find out if free tutoring is offered through the school and if the professors have posted office hours. Can you e-mail questions to professors? Will your questions be answered in a timely fashion? Another consideration is the campus library. Is it easy to find the information you are looking for? Does the school have a special engineering library or carry engineering journals?

Students frequently enjoy joining student chapters of professional organizations. These organizations can be an excellent resource during your college experience and in your career search. Many offer competitions against other colleges. Check to see if the society for the branch of engineering you want to study has student chapters at the schools you are considering. For details about student chapters and their activities, look in the sections of this book about the different branches of engineering.

ACCELERATED PROGRAMS
Certain engineering schools resemble professional schools such as those in law and medicine. They offer undergraduate and graduate degrees in which engineers from industry work on-site to provide training and assistance. Some engineering schools offer a five-year combined undergraduate engineering degree and MBA. Students who want to understand basic management, manufacturing, and large-scale systems engineering and leadership find this combination attractive.

To attract students with an interest in business, some schools are offering Engineering Entrepreneurship Programs. Students with a passion for technological innovation can learn the skills needed to bring high-tech ideas to the marketplace. Using real-world case studies and guest speakers, these popular courses focus on the roles of inventors and founders in successful high-tech startups. Topics usually include evaluating opportunities, shaping products from ideas, intellectual property, gathering resources (people, partners, and capital), high-tech market strategy, leadership in high-tech ventures and, ultimately, harvesting (the various methods for exiting a business).

Programs are designed to prepare students for technology decision making and policy setting as well as for professions outside of engineering. Courses focus on broader skills such as written and oral communications, management, economics, and international relations.

CO-OPS AND INTERNSHIPS

Cooperative education or a co-op experience is one where an engineering student alternates work experience in government, industry or business with academics. For example, a student may do a parallel co-op where they work part-time and go to school part-time or complete a traditional co-op where they work for six months and go to school for six months. A good co-op program may be the perfect answer for the non-traditional student that has financial responsibilities. Some co-ops are non-paid, but provide excellent work experience.

Because a co-op program is longer, the experience you obtain can be more meaningful. Additionally, a co-op experience can show employers you have experience and a solid desire to work in your chosen field. In today's competitive market, you need to do everything possible to make sure you are at the top of your game.

Engineering internships are another way to get your foot in the door. They generally consist of a summer job related to your major at an engineering company. David Tanaka of Pixar Animation Studios began his successful career by interning every summer. By the time he graduated, he was the first choice when a position became available. If you are interested in obtaining an internship position at an engineering firm, find a company you like and apply (send a resume) as early in the school year as possible. Many schools also have a career services program that helps connect students to potential internships and co-ops. These centers can be very good resources for employment during school and after graduation. The early bird usually gets the worm.

Pathways into the Engineering Workforce

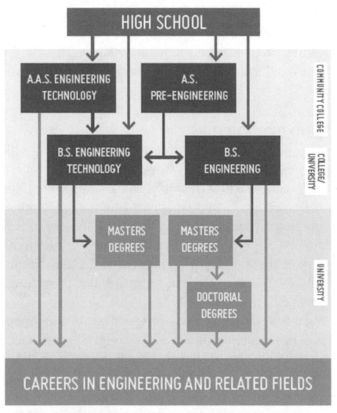

*these are the most **common**, but not the **only** pathways into engineering careers.

Reprinted with permission from the American Society of Mechanical Engineers (ASME)

Chapter 4

Women in Engineering

Susan Knack, a civil engineer for Simpson Gumpertz & Heger, rappels down buildings to examine its construction for various problems or conditions.

Engineering requires creativity, innovation, communication and passion for what you do to communicate ideas; develop tools to interact with family, friends and the environment; and make a difference in the world. We need women in the engineering workforce because women have a unique perspective and approach to solving problems. Women have a long history of using creativity, innovation, tools and materials to solve the problems of feeding, sheltering and clothing their families. For example, weaving can be a highly technical skill, and some of the earliest programmable manufacturing was done on looms.

Smart companies know that to gain a competitive edge in the marketplace, it's important to hire women engineers to design products for women. If design teams are not well-rounded and representative of the population, companies may find that they don't fully understand the problem, design options, or they may not know how to evaluate the constraints and potential solutions. Because of increased global competition and a shortage of women in engineering, it's a good time for women to join the profession. The job opportunities are wide open and many companies are eager to hire women.

Today's U.S. economy depends more than ever on the talents of skilled, high-tech workers. It makes sense because engineers use knowledge, skills and the engineering design process to make stuff — tools, structures, processes — to solve problems. They use available resources such as time, materials and labor to do so. As a group, females are very likely to want to use a tool to do something — solve a problem, make a product, or streamline a process.

Some women have gone even further than that:

- Heather Knight is a pioneer in the growing field of social robotics which investigates ways in which robots could have an impact on our everyday lives. With degrees in electrical engineering and computer science, she is known as a social roboticist and is constantly thinking about new ways to make robots charismatic, giving them the necessary personality and social skills to interact with humans in meaningful ways.

- Dr. Catherine Mohr, a mechanical engineer, is developing the next generation of surgical robots and robotic procedures that allow patients to heal faster and better. She is pushing the boundaries of medicine with her research in robotic-assisted surgery.

- Ada Byron Lovelace collaborated with Charles Babbage, the Englishman credited with inventing the forerunner of the modern computer. She wrote a scientific paper in 1843 that anticipated the development of computer software (including the term software), artificial intelligence, and computer music. The U.S. Department of Defense computer language Ada is named for her.

- Amanda Theodosia Jones invented the vacuum method of food canning, completely changing the entire food processing industry. Before the 1800's, a woman could not get a patent in her own name. A patent was considered property and women could not own property in most states. So, in a move typical of women inventors of the 19th century, Jones denied the idea came from her inventiveness, but rather from instructions received from her late brother from beyond the grave.

- Dr. Angela Moran, a materials engineering scientist, conducts research to help assure that metals and other material that make up some the Navy's most vital equipment (such as aircraft, sea vessels and weaponry) can withstand the stress and demands of their use.

- Mary Engle Pennington revolutionized food delivery with her invention of an insulated train car cooled with ice beds, allowing the long-distance transportation of perishable food for the first time.
- Mary Anderson invented the windshield wiper in 1903. By 1916 they were standard equipment on all American cars.
- Beulah Louise Henry was known as 'the Lady Edison' for the many inventions she patented in the 1920's and 1930's. Her inventions included a bobbinless lockstitch sewing machine, a doll with bendable arms, a vacuum ice cream freezer, a doll with a radio inside, and a typewriter that made multiple copies without carbon paper. Henry founded manufacturing companies to produce her creations and made an enormous fortune in the process.
- Hedy Lamarr was known for her line "Any girl can be glamorous. All you have to do is stand still and look stupid." The 1940's actress invented a sophisticated and unique anti-jamming device for use against Nazi radar. While the U.S. War Department rejected her design, years after her patent had expired, Sylvania adapted the design for a device that today speeds satellite communications around the world. Lamarr received no money, recognition, or credit.
- Grace Murray Hopper, a Rear Admiral in the U.S. Navy, developed COBOL, one of the first high-level computer languages. Hopper is also the person who, upon discovering a moth that had jammed the works of an early computer, popularized the term "bug." In 1991, Hopper became the first woman, as an individual, to receive the National Medal of Technology. One of the Navy's destroyers, the U.S.S. Hopper, is named for her.
- Stephanie Kwoleks discovered a polyamide solvent in 1966 that led to the production of "Kevlar," the crucial component used in canoe hulls, auto bodies and, perhaps most importantly, bulletproof vests.

- Ruth Handler was best known as the inventor of the Barbie doll, also created the first prosthesis for mastectomy patients.
- Dr. Bonnie J. Dunbar helped to develop the ceramic tiles that enable the space shuttle to survive re-entry. In 1985, she had an opportunity to test those tiles first hand as an astronaut aboard the shuttle.

Women often say that the reasons they choose engineering as a career include making a difference in society; having a career that is flexible, enjoyable and rewarding; and knowing that their profession is for "people like me."

Here are just a few examples of what some women are doing with their engineering careers:

- Creating habitats for zoos to keep animals safe and healthy (chemical, mechanical or biomedical engineering).
- Creating new medicines and investigating possible cures for diseases such as cancer (chemical, pharmaceutical or biomedical engineering).
- Creating new prosthetics that would allow a blind person to see (biomedical, computer, optical and electrical engineering).
- Using DNA to solve crimes (biomedical, computer, chemical and genetic engineering).
- Finding new ways to protect the rainforest (biological, agricultural, civil, environmental, computer, mechanical and electrical engineering).
- Developing techniques to make our favorite foods taste better and stay fresh longer (chemical or food and manufacturing and industrial engineering).
- Creating new exhibits and exciting rides for amusement parks (mechanical, civil, structural and electrical engineering).
- Working in the U.S. or in foreign countries to ensure that all people have a safe and healthy water supply (civil and environmental engineering).
- Developing computer programs that help children learn to read, write or communicate (computer, electrical or software engineering).

- Developing new forms of energy to decrease the U.S. dependence on foreign oil (civil, materials, mechanical, electrical, chemical, sustainable and environmental engineering).

According to the American Society of Engineering Education, women took home 18.1% of all bachelor's degrees in 2010. The percentage of bachelor's degrees awarded to women in each discipline were:

- Environmental Engineering (43.1%)
- Biomedical Engineering (37.0%)
- Chemical Engineering (34.5%)
- Agricultural and Biological Engineering (28.8%)
- Industrial/Manufacturing Engineering (30.1%)
- Materials/Metallurgical Engineering (25.4%).
- Architectural Engineering (23.2%)
- Engineering Management (25.6%)
- Civil Engineering (20.3%)
- Electrical Engineering (11.6%)
- Mechanical Engineering (11.5%)

The good news is that young women have good scores on state math tests and are not being outperformed by young men. More young women also graduate from high school and enter college than young men. This means many doors are open wide for women to see all the amazing opportunities in choosing an engineering career. By using teamwork, collaborative problem-solving, and communication skills the career possibilities are almost unlimited. Not only in engineering but also in business, politics, law and medicine – other fields that also benefit from creative problem-solving. Women in engineering can follow their own path and explore numerous ways to better the world.

A great website worth exploring is called Engineer Your Life - a guide to engineering careers for high school girls. Here, you can explore what life and work are like for engineers, see videos of inspiring engineers, and read descriptions of dream engineering jobs. According to www.engineeryourlife.org, ten great reasons you'll love engineering are:

1. Love your work and live your life too — Engineering is an exciting profession, but one of its greatest advantages is that it will leave you time for all the other things in your life that you love!

2. Be creative — Engineering is a great outlet for the imagination and the perfect field for independent thinkers.

3. Work with great people — Engineering takes teamwork, and you'll work with all kinds of people inside and outside the field. Whether they're designers or architects, doctors or entrepreneurs, you'll be surrounded by smart, inspiring people.

4. Solve problems, design things that matter — Come up with solutions no one else has considered. Make your mark on the world.

5. Never be bored — Creative problem solving will take you into uncharted territory, and the ideas of your colleagues will expose you to different ways of thinking. Be prepared to be fascinated and to have your talents stretched in ways you never expected.

6. Make a big salary — Engineers not only earn lots of respect, but they're highly paid. Even the starting salary for an entry-level job is impressive!

7. Enjoy job flexibility — An engineering degree offers you lots of freedom in finding your dream job. It can be a launching pad for jobs in business, design, medicine, law, and government. To employers or graduate schools, an engineering degree reflects a well-educated individual who has been taught ways of analyzing and solving problems that can lead to success in all kinds of fields.

8. Travel — Field work is a big part of engineering. You may end up designing a skyscraper in London or developing safe drinking-water systems in Asia. Or you may stay closer to home, working with a nearby high-tech company or a hospital.

9. Make a Difference — Everywhere you look you'll see examples of engineering having a positive effect on everyday life. Cars are safer, sound systems deliver better acoustics, medical tests are more accurate, and computers and cell phones are a lot more fun! You'll be giving back to your community.

10. Change the world — Imagine what life would be like without pollution controls to preserve the environment, life-saving medical equipment, or low-cost building materials for fighting global poverty. All this takes engineering. In very real and concrete ways, engineers save lives, prevent disease, reduce poverty, and protect our planet.

Chapter 5

Minorities in Engineering

The world population will approach 8 billion people by the year 2020. In the U.S., Hispanic Americans will account for 17 percent of the population, African Americans will account for almost 13 percent, the percentage of white Americans will decrease from 75.6 percent 67.5 percent. By 2050, white Americans will be less than 50 percent of the population (US Census Bureau; 2009 National Population Projections)

As the population demographics change, the engineering workforce must also change. Diversity is essential to good engineering. At the most basic level, men, women, ethnic minorities, racial minorities, and people with disabilities experience the world differently. Those differences in experience are the core or root of creativity and inspiration for each individual. Technological innovation is strongest when the products and services created meet the needs of society. Different cultures bring new ideas to the table and the value of such input should be celebrated. By promoting a healthy and diverse engineering workforce that better reflects the population demographics, we will be able to capture benefits such as an increased standard of living, new career opportunities, increased accessibility to programs and products, and economic prosperity. Advances in medicine, enhanced national security, environmentally sound resource management, and economic growth are all indicators of a healthy and diverse engineering workforce.

Cultures are not always defined by race but can also be a set of shared values, attitudes and goals. The popularity of Instant Messaging (IM), text messaging, social networks and chat rooms are also considered a culture. These communication styles were popularized by a younger generation that was catering to their differences in thinking and behavior. In the U.S. in 2009, 286 million people sent 5.09 billion text messages per day. Studies have also found that more teens have used IM for homework than for dating. To meet the needs of a diverse society, we must train a diverse variety of engineers who understand communication preferences and the social and political motivations or movements of cultures around the world.

Ever since a 1970s study by the National Science Foundation showed that ethnic minorities (with the exception of Asian Americans) were vastly underrepresented in engineering, the profession has made efforts to recruit minorities. Various programs now exist to acquaint minority students, their families and teachers with the field as well as to mentor and support minority engineering students. Camps, competitions and scholarships specifically target minorities; colleges have established minorities in engineering or diversity in engineering programs; and many employers have diversity or multicultural departments. Though the rates of enrollment have increased, actual numbers of minority engineers are still low.

According to the American Society for Engineering Education (ASEE), the percentage of bachelor's degrees awarded by ethnicity in 2010 were:

- African American (4.5%)
- Hispanic American (7.0%)
- Asian American (12.2%)
- Other (1.2%)
- White (69.8%)

Two major societies support minorities in engineering:
1. The National Society of Black Engineers (NSBE) - founded in 1975, is the premier organization serving African Americans in engineering and technology. With more than 30,000 members and 300 chapters in the U.S. and abroad, NSBE supports and promotes the aspirations of college and pre-college students and technical professionals. NSBE's mission is "to increase the number of culturally responsible Black engineers who excel academically, succeed professional and positively impact the community."

2. The Society of Hispanic Professional Engineers (SHPE) -
   founded in Los Angeles, California, in 1974 by a group of
   engineers employed by the city of Los Angeles. They are the
   premier organization serving the Hispanic community. Their
   objective was to form a national organization of professional
   engineers to serve as role models in the Hispanic community.
   Their mission states, "SHPE changes lives by empowering
   the Hispanic community to realize their fullest potential and
   impacts the world through STEM awareness, access, support
   and development."

Chapter 6

"Wow!" Careers in Engineering

With an increase in technology in our daily lives, many people now view engineering as a marketable skill. Many newly emerging non-technical fields need the logical problem-solving abilities of engineers.

Not every engineer craves the traditional engineering path. Diverse and plentiful opportunities exist for the educated non-mainstream engineer. Opportunities such as the Peace Corps, Engineers Without Borders, imagineering, music engineering, sports engineering, green and alternative energy engineering, inventing and entrepreneurship are only a handful of the possibilities. Engineers also work in law, medicine, teaching, finance, writing, politics, sales, and business because their analytical and logical thinking skills are an asset in almost every industry.

Peace Corps

John F. Kennedy introduced the Peace Corps program in 1960 during his campaign for the presidency. The Peace Corps offers a peaceful way to work for your country. The purpose of the program is to teach transferable skills that can be used to help people long after you are back at home. Today, Peace Corps volunteers serve in more than 90 countries.

Employers want recruits who have an appreciation of diversity, adaptability, and a global perspective. The Peace Corps offers a personal experience in living and thinking about the world from a different cultural and environmental perspective. It enables new engineers to take on more responsibility and obtain more practical experience than recent college graduates would normally have. For a closer look at an engineer in the Peace Corps, see the article about Charles Wright in the section on environmental engineering.

The Peace Corps offers the opportunity for civil, mechanical, structural, sanitary, architectural, or environmental engineers to train people to develop comprehensive city or town plans; improve water, sanitation, and transportation systems; and construct roads, hospitals, and municipal buildings. Graduates from other branches of engineering are also sought to teach math or science to school children.

"The toughest job you'll ever love" is the Peace Corps' motto. The adventure begins with eight to twelve weeks of language training, most often in your host country, where you will stay for two years. During that time you will gain valuable professional and hands-on experience with all expenses paid.

Peace Corps volunteers returning to the U.S. are given a professional edge. They receive first choice for government jobs and a readjustment allowance for the time spent as volunteers.

Engineers Without Borders

Engineers Without Borders (EWB) leads projects to improve the quality of life for people all over the world. In 2002, Bernard Amadei founded Engineers Without Borders (ewb-usa.org), a Boulder, Colorado nonprofit organization, to support community-driven development programs across the globe. Engineers design and implement sustainable engineering projects to help bring essential provisions such as food and water to less fortunate villages and communities. EWB now has more than 12,000 members working in 48 countries on 400 projects. Amadei sees "huge opportunities for doing well by doing good" by empowering the world's poor "in a respectful way where we create capacity at the local level."

Daniel Saulnier, a civil engineer from Boston helped a small village in the mountains of Honduras in Central America build a system of pipes and tanks to bring clean drinking water to their homes. Before the project, villagers had to hike down to a polluted river and carry buckets of dirty water back uphill to their homes. They were often sick and malnourished because of the poor water quality, and young children would often die. Now they open faucets in their front yards and get cool, clean spring water. They are healthier and happier, and have extra water for growing vegetables.

Saulnier said, "construction of the project was a team effort between the group of us from EWB and the people living in the village.
We contributed technical equipment and engineering knowledge, and they contributed local know-how and a seemingly endless supply of hard work. The entire project, including two miles of trench for the pipeline, was constructed by hand, using picks and shovels and muscles. We spent our evenings doing engineering calculations, planning construction activities, and figuring out solutions to new problems that kept cropping up. We spent our days working  from sunrise to sunset, hiking up mountains in 95°F heat, climbing through barbed wire fences, hauling pipes, tools and surveying equipment around, and trying to learn Spanish. We would stop for a lunch of bean burritos and water, and would often be sitting on the side of a hill, looking at the rolling green mountains surrounding us, and chatting with each other and our new Honduran friends. We learned a lot about the way many people in the world lead their lives, from the challenges of poverty and lack of educational opportunity to the pleasures of living off the land and being surrounded by close family ties."

Imagineering

Have you ever wondered who designed and constructed the theme parks around the world? One trip to Disney World or Disneyland can leave the most reserved of us awestruck and filled with wonder. Imagineers are responsible for designing all aspects of theme parks. These engineers attempt to merge science and art to create illusion that is so close to reality that your mind can't distinguish it from the real thing.

Amusement parks offer only thrill rides such as roller coasters, tea cups and water slides. Theme parks are different—they envelop visitors in a seemingly different time and place based on a story or theme. For example, Space Mountain is a ride at Disneyland that tries to make people believe they are in space, when actually, they are riding a roller coaster inside a man-made mountain.

Walt Disney opened Disneyland, the first theme park, on July 17, 1955. Imagineering, a term coined by Walt Disney in 1962, refers to the work of a team of people who design theme parks. Team members include illustrators, architects, interior designers, industrial designers, graphic designers, and, of course, engineers. According to Nate Naversen at Imagination Enterprises, "Engineers figure out a way to make it work. Whether it be sizing the structural columns and measuring shear forces on a roller coaster, or developing new electronics to make an animatronic character function, engineers do the math to make everything 'stand up.' Structural and mechanical engineering are the most common majors."

How do they do it? Imagineers attempt to stimulate all five senses: sight, hearing, touch, smell, and taste. A sixth sense, imagination, is also stimulated to transport guests to the magical story world created by the imagineers. The more senses that are enveloped simultaneously, the more real the fantasy world appears.

Imagination is the sixth sense because, without it, the other senses would have less emphasis. Take a look at how each sense is stimulated. A whole team of people may work together to appeal to only one aspect of one sense. For example, the imagineers who manage visual aspects include the architects, landscapers, and lighting engineers. Imagineers who manage audio aspects design the music to suggest a mood. (Remember the music in the last scary movie you saw?) There are also imagineers who manage touch, smell, and taste. Typically, if the story or theme of the attraction can convince people they are in a faraway place or time, the attraction is truly marvelous.

Merging art and science to create amazing theme parks is different from engineering in any other medium. The result of your work is people oriented rather than technology oriented. Engineers love to fully harness the capabilities of technology but in this industry, along with the perfectly executed animatronic characters and innovative technology, the guest experience must always come first.

For more information about imagineering, preparing to work as an entertainment engineer, and the future of themed attraction design, pick up a copy of *The Fantastical Engineer: A Thrillseeker's Guide to Careers in Theme Park Engineering.*

Sports Equipment Design

Sports engineering is an excellent way to impact athletes, sports and businesses around the world. Engineers in this field are some of the most dynamic, innovative and creative engineers on the planet. Not

only is this industry full of diverse, fun and intriguing opportunities, but most of the engineers working in the sporting goods industry became engineers because they love sports and wanted to either increase their performance or enhance the sport overall. A company that wants to design a new swimsuit for Olympic athletes would prefer to hire an engineer who swims. A company

that wants to design a new baseball bat would prefer to hire an engineer who plays baseball. A company that is designing high-performance mountain bikes would prefer to hire an engineer who has a keen interest in bike design or races bicycles. The industry offers some awesome careers for athletically inclined engineers!

For example, chemical and materials engineers will find a wealth of employment in the athletic shoe industry. Constantly on the lookout for new materials for soles and outer coverings, shoe manufacturers are in ongoing competition for the best cushioning, lightest overall design, most comfortable and best traction products. Finding new materials that add "breathability" for the long distance runner, springiness for basketball players, increased traction for skateboarders, flexibility and grip for wrestlers, more cushioning for long jumpers and/or strength and comfort for skeleton racers can make the shoe industry a challenging and rewarding field for an athletically minded engineer.

On a pair of athletic shoes:

- Mechanical engineers may design systems for manufacturing, motion analysis or impact testing and be involved in building and/or testing prototypes.
- Biomedical engineers may design systems for motion analysis and biomechanical analysis of injuries, stress patterns, or kinesthetic optimization.
- Chemical, materials or textile engineers may develop or design new soles, fabrics or other materials for shoes.
- Manufacturing engineers may design systems or processes for manufacturing shoes more efficiently.
- Computer engineers may design software or hardware to aid in pressure or impact detection analysis, manufacturing processes or information systems.
- Industrial engineers may maintain the bill of materials and routing information, cost standards and recommend pricing for new products. Or, they may be involved in learning about and training on manufacturing techniques.

For more information about sports engineering or preparing to work as a sports engineer, pick up a copy of *High Tech Hot Shots: Careers in Sports Engineering*.

Music Engineering

Music, audio, electrical, and computer engineers are a major component of a team of people who create iPods, digital instruments, microphones, speakers, headphones, Internet music sites such as iTunes, theatre sound, and live concert sound. They work in music studios, for video game companies, cell phone companies and for other software companies that need audio support. They focus on revolutionizing the  music and sound industries and finding new ways to listen to, create, store and preserve music (i.e., music on iPods, cell phones, etc.).

There are many approaches to combining engineering, technology and music. In general, a career in music engineering or technology requires that a student be musically inclined as well as technical and creative. If they love music, like to work on computers, are fascinated by electronics and mechanics, or have a love for gadgets, combining music with engineering or technology may be the solution to a satisfying career. Not only can it lead to a successful career contributing to the newest releases on the charts, but it can also lead to success creating instruments or changing the way we listen to music. The good news is this field is wide open with plenty of opportunities for a hard working, ambitious person.

Students can get a formal engineering degree, certificate or degree in music engineering technology, or they can be self-taught. They can go to school for four or more years, two years, one year, one month, one week or one hour. Whatever their passion and ambition, there is an accessible career path. The most common majors for music engineers are audio, electrical, computer and software engineering.

For more information about music engineering and preparing to work as a music engineer, pick up a copy of *The Musical Engineer: A Music Enthusiast's Guide to Careers in Engineering and Technology.*

Green Energy Engineering

Each of us uses energy everyday. Not only do we use energy to walk, talk, play sports, and function (all of which use calories) but we also use energy to power our cars, toast our bread, watch TV, on so on. Energy is everywhere and there are multiple forms of it. Energy can be kinetic (electrical, thermal, geothermal, nuclear, light, motion, water or sound energy) or potential (chemical, nuclear or stored energy). When energy is renewable it means that it can be re-used.  For example, energy from the sun can provide power when it hits a solar panel. The sun's energy is renewable because the energy from the sun is still available even after you use it (Newton's First Law of Thermodynamics states that energy cannot be created or destroyed. It can only be transferred from one form to another.) If the same power was being provided by natural gas, once you use the gas, it is gone forever because natural gas is a non-renewable energy source.

Engineers are hard at work designing ways we can use renewable energy. Engineers in this industry are designing engines that run cleaner for improved efficiency as well as developing electric and hybrid vehicle batteries and systems. Other engineers are working to improve the efficiency of wind, water and solar power. Still other engineers are exploring the potential of future technologies utilizing wind, solar, geothermal, biofuel and wave energy sources. These need to be cultivated, expanded and implemented, as well as meeting the increased demand for greener buildings and transportation systems.

Jobs in the green collar sector — such as solar panel and turbine manufacturing, installation, sales, research, and design are in high demand. Renewable energy technologies diversify our energy supply, reduce our dependence on imported fuels, improve air quality, offset greenhouse gas emissions and stimulate the economy. The opportunities in this sector are blossoming and will provide tremendous job security for engineers. It's a great time to be a green energy engineer.

For more information about green engineering, pick up a copy of *The Green Engineer: Engineering Careers to Save the Earth.*

Space Engineering

If you think you'd enjoy working as an astronaut, going on spacewalks and building rockets, the good news is that you can be almost any type of engineer. NASA employs nine engineers for every scientist. They hire biomedical engineers to make space suits, chemical engineers to help with life support systems, mechanical engineers to work on almost everything, electrical engineers to work on control systems, etc. There are endless opportunities for students in this field and you don't have to narrow your interests to succeed. According to "Reliable Robots" on the Futures Channel, some engineers might spend their days "fine tuning a set of million dollar micro-cameras so the rovers can 'see' better while exploring miles of Martian terrain." Or, they might be "designing tele-operated mini-rovers in an office that looks more like a high tech R&D lab at a toy company than a NASA research facility."

Dr. Sally Ride gave great advice to students. She said, "The most important steps that I followed were studying math and science in school. I think the advice that I would give to any kids who want to be astronauts is to make sure that they realize that NASA is looking for people with a whole variety of backgrounds: they are looking for medical doctors, microbiologists, geologists, physicists, electrical engineers. So find something that you really like and then pursue it as far as you can and NASA is apt to be interested in that profession."

NASA's engineers brought us inventions such as the hand held vacuum cleaner, the firefighter breathing apparatus, safer runways, storm warning systems, better sunglasses, car crash technology, freeze dried meals, baby food, improved air quality, artificial limbs and much, much more. Engineers at NASA help our daily life in ways that often go unrecognized.

The NASA website is full of information to help you explore space. Watch videos of the shuttle launch and even see it from a camera on the solid rocket boosters. There are numerous pictures and it's easy to get information by visiting www.nasa.gov.

Engineering for Animal Health

Engineering medical equipment and life support systems for animals is a big field for engineers. Each year, Americans spend billions of dollars on their pets. Pet care is a booming industry and a fantastic field for engineers. Many students are drawn to the field with the hope of helping both small and large animals. Engineers are responsible for building all new exhibits for endangered or rare animals such as a tiger. They ensure the animal is happy in its new home, that the animal cannot escape from its habitat and that the guests have a nice viewing area without encroaching on the tiger's personal space. To do this, engineers need information such as how high a tiger jumps, what's the perfect climate and do tigers like other tigers. Once the information is compiled, they can design an exhibit that will make the tiger happy.

Zoo design is a tricky business. It's interesting to learn about penguins, hippos, rhinos, giraffes, etc. The work is similar to designing building systems but the equipment used in a zoo is unusual. Engineers usually receive special training, so important for them to keep up with the changes in the industry. Not only do engineers have to research and design the perfect type of environment for each animal, they also have to keep the zoo visitors happy by creating something that is aesthetically pleasing. Zoos spend money to obtain new animals and build exhibits in order to attract more guests and stay in business.

Architects usually design the face/aesthetics of the zoo but engineers are required to keep the animals alive and healthy. Engineers who work for zoos are called life support engineers and are usually educated in architectural, civil, chemical, biomedical, environmental and mechanical engineering.

Engineering in Business

A practical knowledge of business is becoming increasingly important as more engineers become involved with start-up companies. Engineering schools help students develop entrepreneurial skills such as dealing with venture capitalists, writing business plans, and understanding the business processes of a company. Students have to understand not only what it takes to technically create an invention but the financial and marketing aspects of their invention as well.

Engineers are also needed in business because they comprehend and manage large scale issues. For example, if a new product is developed that initially requires a raw material, the engineer might research and find that the needed raw material is a limited resource and the company may run out of their ingredient in the near future, making the business model unsustainable. The engineer may be able to locate alternative materials that are sustainable and offer fewer environmental impacts.

Inventing Products

Engineers of all types have a wildly successful history of entrepreneurial ventures. Some engineers seem to be born inventors. They seem to have innate knowledge about how to be more efficient, make things easier to use, create new products, or save money. Almost everything you see around you was invented by someone.

Inventing a product can mean starting your own company or simply selling your idea and design. If you sell your idea and design, you can expect the buying company to pay for the manufacturing and all promotion while you collect a royalty or lump-sum payment.

If you start your own company, you will be responsible for manufacturing and marketing your product. The good side of starting your own company is that you will retain control of your design and make money too. The bad side is that you need to come up with front money to manufacture your product.

FEATURE ARTICLE

INVENT IT TODAY!

Have you ever seen a toy, game or gizmo and thought: "I could have invented that?" Or, have you said or heard someone say: "I had that idea years ago. They stole my idea!" Many people have had these experiences because they have good ideas, but few people are willing to make them work. The few who do are called inventors.

If you have creative ideas you can make a nice living as an inventor. Having the training of an engineer helps you transform ideas into working devices. The great thing is that you don't have to wait; you can start today.

You know enough about the products and services that kids and families use that you can think of better ways. Keep a notebook of your ideas. Inventors call their notebooks "Inventor's Logs." Not only do these help you remember your creative ideas, they also can be used to prove that you came up with the idea before someone else did.

Your inventor's log should be a bound book of blank pages. Draw your ideas and describe them in words. Sign and date the pages and have a friend sign the pages too. If your friend signs and understands what your idea is, his or her testimony in court can help you win any legal battles over who owns the invention.

The inventor's log is your first line of defense. If you think your invention will sell, you might consider getting a patent. However, patents are expensive and you don't want to spend the time or money getting one until you are convinced you'll get the money back in selling or licensing your invention. There are lots of tricky rules on patents so it will help you to read up on them.

As important as protecting your ideas is, it's even more important to make them work and to do market research. You need to find out if someone else has a product that is the same as the one you're working on. It's common for people not to know about similar products. After all, there are hundreds of thousands of products created in the U.S. alone and no one person knows them all. So, you need to talk to people who know that type of product. You could ask sales people in stores that might carry it. If you can find companies that manufacture similar or related products you could talk to them. You will need to tell them enough about your invention so they can think about similar ideas. But, to protect your ideas, you don't want to tell them everything about it.

If you find that there are no existing products

like your invention on the market, you can start working to make a mock up of your invention. You need to make a working model to prove that it works and so you can show other people. Most people quit at this point as they think that making something is too hard. But here is where you persistence and your engineering skills pay off. If you don't know how to make part of it, you can find experts in your community to help you. If you are persistent, you will succeed.

One of the great things about being an inventor is that you're always learning. You may need to learn how to use a new tool or a new material. Inventors, like other creative people, are eager and curious learners, because everything they learn may help them solve a problem and complete an invention.

Will you make a zillion dollars as inventor? Most inventors don't hit the jackpot. But they have a lot of fun doing what they enjoy. Think how they feel — or think how you'd feel — if you saw a product in a store that you had invented.

So take that inventive idea of yours and get to work. The world may be waiting for your widget.

Reprinted with permission from Ed Sobey, Ph.D.,
President of the Northwest Invention Center and author
of "Inventing Stuff."

Engineers in Politics

Engineers can also be found in all levels of government trying to shape and mold public policy. Three engineers even became president of the United States!

- George Washington, the 1st president was known for his contributions to the surveying field and was considered a civil engineer.
- Herbert Hoover, the 31st president of the United States graduated from Stanford University in 1891 with a degree

in mining engineering. He went to China and worked for a private corporation as China's leading engineer. Hoover is known for the Hoover dam that has his name, not only because it was built during his presidential term but because his direct involvement in the engineering problems it had. The dam was first called Boulder Canyon Dam.

* Jimmy Carter, the 39th president of the United States, attended Georgia Tech and the U.S. Naval Academy. He served in the navy as an engineer working with nuclear-powered submarines, and later retired to manage the family's peanut farming business.

FEATURE ARTICLE

GEORGE WASHINGTON - THE FIRST U.S. ENGINEER

A gentleman farmer of inherited wealth and limited formal education, Washington acquired credible surveying skills early in life, but excelled as a manager, strategist, and leader.

Washington directed a growing nation toward technical advancements, invention, and education. He promoted construction of roads, canals, the Capitol, docks and ports, water works, and new efforts to extract coal and ores and develop manufacturing resources.

Around the world, technology was gaining equal footing with pure science. Washington's contemporaries included James Watt (Scottish steam-engine inventor); Joseph Priestley (British chemistry pioneer); Richard Arkwright (British cotton-spinning inventor); John Fitch (American steamboat inventor); and the Montgolfier brothers (French aeronauts).

First in Washington's heart, it seems, was agriculture. As a young surveyor, his first sight of the Shenandoah Valley reportedly inspired the vision of an agricultural empire. As an adult, Washington settled into Mt. Vernon as a tobacco planter and experimented with the innovative agricultural techniques of crop rotation, soil fertilization, and livestock management. He had accurately predicted the valley's fertile farming potential.

As the foremost American general, Washington promoted at least one engineering marvel ahead of its time. During the Revolutionary War, he sent David Bushnell's hand-operated submarine into New York Harbor to sink a British warship. The Turtle's lone operator attempted to attach a timed bomb to the British Eagle's hull. The mission failed when the bomb floated away before exploding. The technology just wasn't advanced enough for Washington's vision, and submarines didn't become a force in navies for the next 100 years.

On June 9, 1778, at Valley Forge, Pennsylvania, General George Washington issued a call for engineers and engineering education. This order is considered the genesis of a U.S Army Engineer School, which found its permanent home at Fort Belvoir, Virginia, where Washington had practiced surveying. As President (1789-97), Washington pushed for the passage of the first U.S. Patent Act in 1789, and signed the first official U.S. patent to Samuel Hopkins of Vermont for his process of making potash and pearl ashes. In 1794, President Washington established a Corps of Artillerists and Engineers to be educated and stationed at West Point in New York, which later become the U.S. Military Academy at West Point.

From transportation to education, Washington's engineering vision proved to be ahead of its time. After his death in 1799, many of the technologies he supported provided an impetus to the American Industrial Revolution. New York's Erie Canal (1817-25) was built, and canals soon crisscrossed America east of the Mississippi. By the 1830's, the nation's population tripled, traveling west through canals, along rivers, and across new roads and bridges. The Army Corps of Engineers began many of these projects.

By the middle of the century, the railroads

become the favored mode of transportation. As a result, America had gone west and Washington's vision was realized.

Reprinted courtesy of the American Society of Mechanical Engineers.

The Bachelor of Art in Engineering

Many newly emerging non-technical fields need the logical problem-solving abilities of engineers. The Bachelor of Art (BA) in Engineering is considered to be the liberal arts degree for a technologically driven society. Most BA programs in engineering are designed to appeal to a broader segment of the population than the BS degree. The degree is usually interdisciplinary and graduates of these programs may find themselves working in public policy, management, business or any other sector of society that can benefit from a thorough grounding in the engineering process. The Bachelor of Art is a way to fuse engineering with a liberal arts education. However, because of the liberal arts emphasis, graduates with a BA in engineering do not qualify for a professional engineering license.

Part II

The Many Faces of Engineering

Engineering is a diverse and challenging field of study. Not all engineering students are alike, and the engineering marketplace is no different. With more than 50 major branches of engineering and engineering technology, and over 100 specialties, there is something for everyone who pursues these fields. Your personal goals, skills, and personality will determine which branch or specialty of engineering is right for you.

See the appendix for a list of all of the engineering and engineering technology ABET accredited programs of study.

Salary Information

The median income cited within each discipline comes from the U.S. Department of Labor, Bureau of Labor Statistics. The starting salary cited for each discipline described comes from the National Association of Colleges and Employers report.

Respondents represented all branches of engineering, a variety of industries and job functions, and differing registration status; they were males and females of various racial and ethnic origins from across the United States.

Many factors affect income. For example, your salary will reflect your level of education and years of work experience as well as your job function. Some regions such as New York and California typically pay more to compensate for their high cost of living. Salaries also vary from one industry to another and from one branch of engineering to another (See the following pages to determine which branch pays the most.) Salaries may also vary depending on your gender and other factors.

AERONAUTICAL / AEROSPACE ENGINEERING

MEDIAN STARTING SALARY: $64,200
MEDIAN INCOME: $104,810

Aeronautical/aerospace engineers design and develop technology for commercial aviation, national defense, and space exploration. They may help design and manufacture military aircraft, missiles, and spacecraft. Within this field, they may specialize in the structure of the aircraft, aerodynamics, guidance and control, propulsion and design, manufacturing, or a certain type of aircraft. Commercial airliners, military aircraft, space  shuttles, satellites, rockets, and helicopters are all within reach for talented aeronautical engineers, who may also be referred to as astronautical, aviation, or rocket engineers.

Aeronautical/aerospace engineers work on the hundreds of satellites that orbit the earth and on the commercial and military aircraft that carry millions of passengers. Other areas of focus include developing materials that can withstand extreme temperatures, investigating biological implications of astronauts in space, and reducing the effects of sonic booms on the environment.

From the Wright brothers back in 1903 to the international space stations of today, aeronautical/aerospace engineering has enjoyed tremendous growth. The need for quieter, more fuel-efficient and alternative fuel commercial airplanes as well as the increased demand for spacecraft and helicopters will create many opportunities for aeronautical engineers. It is a very progressive and complex field that will undoubtedly continue to advance as we attempt to travel beyond the moon and explore the planets.

The automotive and sports science industries also need aeronautical engineers. All fifty states require registration of engineers whose work may affect lives, health, or property and engineers who offer their services to the public. Hence, professional registration is especially important for aeronautical/ aerospace engineers. You can learn more about aeronautical/ aerospace engineering by visiting the Aerospace Engineering Division website of the ASME at www.asme.org.

FEATURE ARTICLE

AEROSPACE GRAD MAKING HIS MARK ON THE GAME OF GOLF -- AND ON THE GOLF BALL

Bob Thurman works in a world of dimples and bluff bodies. No, he's not a high-fashion photographer or a Hollywood producer. Thurman, an aerospace engineer, designs golf balls for Wilson Sporting Goods at the company's Humboldt, Tenn., research and testing facility.

While Humboldt may be a long way from the fashion runways of Rome and the soundstages of Hollywood, it is also far removed from the aircraft plants and NASA facilities where you would expect to find an aerospace engineer.

For Thurman, the road to Humboldt-and a career designing golf balls for a major sporting goods manufacturer-began in his hometown of Dyersburg, Tennessee.

"When I was in high school, I really loved math and science and knew I wanted to go into some type of engineering," he explained. "When I applied to MSU, I went down the list of engineering programs and aerospace sounded the best, even though I never was a big airplane buff."

Thurman worked with Martin Marietta Corporation in New Orleans as a cooperative education student following his freshman year. At that time, the company was building fuel tanks for the space shuttle. It was exciting work for an engineering student, but it also was somewhat discouraging.

"I learned a lot, but I also saw that there were several hundred engineers working on the same project," he said. "It was not the kind of environment where I felt like I could make a dent."

Returning to campus the next fall, Thurman discovered an aspect of aerospace engineering that was more appealing to him than working on huge projects with hundreds of other engineers.

"The first time I walked into Dr. Koenig's lab, I knew I had found what I wanted to do," he explained, referring to research on baseball bats and other athletic equipment being conducted by aerospace engineering professor Keith Koenig.

Although Koenig's work fired his imagination, Thurman also was involved in some of the more traditional activities for aerospace engineering students, including work on a student space plane project.

After receiving his bachelor's degree, Thurman was headed for graduate school, until fate stepped in.

"I needed a summer job. My father works for a company that sells raw materials to the Wilson golf ball plant in Humboldt and he suggested I send the company a resume," he noted.

The resume made its way to Wilson's U.S. headquarters in Chicago at the same time the company was in the process of decentralizing its research and development operations. As part of the plan, an engineer was needed to design and test balls and other golf equipment at the Tennessee facility. Thurman was hired, and he's been seeking a better golf ball ever since.

"My first day on the job, I pulled out one of my aerodynamics textbooks and found one page with a reference to something like a golf ball," he said.

That doesn't mean he wasn't prepared, though.

"Engineering school teaches you how to solve problems," he said. "They can't teach you everything, but they can provide you with a good, sound foundation. When it comes to particular applications, you go back and recall the things you've learned."

One of the things Thurman learned at Mississippi State is that a round sphere, a golf ball for example, is called a bluff body and is a complicated object when it comes to aerodynamics.

"Even though an airplane may be pitching or rolling, the geometry is basically very static and under the influence of powered flight," he says. "The flight of a golf ball is different. After leaving the club face, the ball immediately begins to slow down and the spin begins to decay as well."

The dimples, those little indentations on the surface of a golf ball, help it in its flight from tee to hole. "With a golf ball, the dimples actually create turbulence, which keeps the airflow attached to the ball, producing a smaller wake and reduced aerodynamic drag," said Thurman. "With a smooth ball the wake separates much earlier from the ball, creating a large wake and tremendous drag forces."

He added that three primary factors determine the performance of a golf ball-the amount of surface covered by dimples, the angle that a dimple breaks from the surface of the ball, and dimple depth.

"The maximum amount of the surface that can be covered with dimples is about 80 percent," he explains. "Changes in how sharp the angle is where the dimple breaks from the surface of the ball and dimple depth provide room for the most variables."

As a general rule of thumb, deeper dimples produce lower, flatter trajectories. Shallow dimples produce higher, ballooning trajectories. The key, Thurman says, is to create a dimple with enough depth to produce air turbulence around the ball as it rotates in flight. That helps the ball penetrate what engineers call "the force barrier"-the resistance that builds up as the ball moves through the air.

Thurman works in an office adjoining the lab. Baskets of balls covered with lines, dots, and other felt-pen markings fill some corners in the office. With a few strokes on his computer keyboard, the engineer can bring up the image of his latest creation on the computer screen. Horizontal and vertical lines that map a new dimple pattern dissect the computer image of a golf ball.

What's the perfect number of dimples? It is possible to design a ball with 1,000 or more dimples, Thurman said, but he's designed a 500-dimple ball that's been very successful in Wilson's Staff Titanium and Ultra 500 lines.

"I wasn't trying to develop a 500-dimple ball," he explained. "It just took 500 to properly define the pattern." He added that a properly dimpled ball will go about 250 yards, while with a smooth ball you would be lucky to get 120 yards.

There are a lot of options when it comes to dimple patterns for golf balls. Finding the best options is part of Thurman's job as Wilson's principal engineer of aerodynamics and manager of the company's golf research testing function. He's been very successful at that job, as noted by the two U.S. patents for golf ball designs hanging on the walls of his office.

But it's not a job where you can rest on your laurels. "Most companies come out with one or two new golf ball designs each year," said Thurman. "Ball designs that were in production four years ago are no longer being produced."

Manufacturers must adhere to certain weight and size standards established by the U.S. Golf Association. Dimple design and other factors can, however, be used to customize balls for different types of players.

"You have balls manufactured for higher handicapped players that are primarily just for distance," Thurman noted. "Tour players, on the other hand, are not as concerned about distance as they are with the feel of the ball and the ability to control it on the green."

Wilson and other manufacturers produce balls that fit the needs of players at all points along the handicap spectrum, as well as customized balls for special events, promotions, and to fit the preferences of players in Japan and other countries.

The diversified demand will likely keep Bob Thurman busy for years to come, and it's a prospect he looks forward to.

"When you go to the best courses in this country or even overseas and you see someone playing with that little golf ball that started in this computer here in Humboldt, that makes this a great job!"

Reprinted with the permission of Mississippi State University.

AGRICULTURAL AND BIOLOGICAL ENGINEERING

MEDIAN STARTING SALARY: $68,000
MEDIAN INCOME: $77,370

One in seven people around the world is suffering from hunger. By 2025, 2.8 billion people will be facing fresh water shortages. Our population places great demand on our limited natural resources.

If you want to be a part of the solution, agricultural and biological engineering (A&BE) is a great choice. A&BEs work to ensure that we have the necessities of life: safe and plentiful food to eat, pure water to drink, clean fuel and energy sources and a safe, healthy environment in which to live.

Agricultural and biological engineering, two closely integrated disciplines often called biological systems (biosystems), bioresources, or natural resources engineering, are concerned with finding solutions for life on a small planet. As an agricultural engineer, you will create new technology for agricultural systems, materials, and products that will help provide high-quality and affordable food and fiber for the world's billions. Every aspect of food production, processing, marketing, and distribution can benefit from your expertise.

A&BEs devise practical, efficient solutions for producing, storing, transporting, processing, and packaging agricultural products. They solve problems related to systems, processes and machines that interact with humans, plants, animals, microorganisms and biological materials. They develop solutions for responsible, innovative uses of agricultural products, byproducts and wastes; and of our natural resources, including soil, water, air and energy. And they do all this with a constant eye toward improved protection of people, animals and the environment.

Agricultural and Biological Engineers may:
- Find new uses for agricultural products, byproducts, and waste.
- Develop industrial air filters embedded with microorganisms that help reduce air pollution.
- Determine improved methods of soil erosion control.
- Study animal behavior to develop more humane housing environments, and/or
- Develop renewable energy sources from grain oils.

You would enjoy a career in A&BE if you want to work with people, help make a more sustainable future, have a "green" focus, enjoy working with plants or animals and enjoy good food.

There are currently 40 accredited colleges of engineering that teach A&BE. However, there are no longer any programs that are solely agricultural. The field has evolved to be much broader and that allows more career flexibility. If this career sounds right for you, be sure to contact a few schools that teach it to get an even more comprehensive understanding of your possibilities.

FEATURE ARTICLE

OCEANS OF OPPORTUNITY

As a boy growing up in Nanjing, China, Jaw-Kai Wang had never heard of an agricultural engineer. But a professor at National Taiwan University changed all that when he made Wang an offer he couldn't refuse. "If you want to save the world, this is where you begin," the professor said. Those words lured Wang into the program at the university where he would later graduate with a bachelor's degree in agricultural engineering. He then relocated to the United States and continued his education at Michigan State University where he earned a master's degree and Ph.D. in agricultural engineering. He is now professor of biosystems engineering at the University of Hawaii. After teaching agricultural machine design for several years, Wang's interests turned from land to water. In the late 1970's, one of his graduate students began a project to study prawns, which are edible crustaceans that resemble shrimp. Wang secured funding to start and maintain an "aquaculture" program at the school. Since then, he has made major breakthroughs in raising shrimp and oysters for mass production and is developing some innovative uses for algae. "We are agricultural engineers," Wang says. "What we do best is to grow things. To produce things from biological systems." By 1989, Wang had developed a way to improve oyster and shrimp production. He designed an aquaculture system for raising shrimp and prawns and soon noticed a water quality problem caused by a buildup of uneaten food and shrimp droppings. He found that he could put algae, which feeds on the wastes, in the water with the shrimp.

When the water is clean, the algae is pumped into a separate tank housing oysters. Because the algae floats, Wang designed a fluidized bed to float the oysters on a column of water. The oysters can then eat the algae. This system is patented and a company in Hawaii is using it. Currently, Wang is working toward getting a patent on an antibiotic made from algae. The drug, which kills infection-causing bacteria such as staphylococcus, is being tested on animals and could someday be used against bacteria that has become resistant to existing drugs. Wang says algae has many other uses, including as a food coloring. "People have never bothered much to look at it," he says. "There is nothing but potential here. It's so interesting." Wang predicts that within the next 10 years, jobs in aquaculture will be plentiful as fish production becomes important as a food source. He believes that an agricultural and biological engineering background allows people entering this field to be versatile in these areas. At 65, Wang says "there's never a dull moment" in his career. "You put the puzzle together piece by piece."

There will always be a need for production from biological systems." And as for saving the world: "There is still the idealistic part," he says. "To do something useful. To make a contribution. That you should give back to society."

Reprinted from Resources Magazine published by the American Society of Agricultural and Biological Engineers.

Some A&BEs may work on developing nontoxic pesticides; others may work on developing stronger and more efficient farm equipment such as tractors. Still others may develop instruments to test the safety of food and water supplies. High-tech agricultural engineers may work on computer systems to automate large farms. Visit the American Society for Agricultural and Biological Engineers (ASABE) website at asabe.org for more information.

ARCHITECTURAL ENGINEERING

MEDIAN STARTING SALARY (FOR CIVIL ENGINEERING): $51,793
MEDIAN INCOME (FOR CIVIL ENGINEERING): $84,140

Architectural engineering, according to the National Society of Architectural Engineers (NSAE), is "the application of engineering principles to the design of technical systems of buildings."

Do you have the ability to be analytical as well as creative? Can you think systematically and pragmatically, and then turn around and be creative and spontaneous? If so, architectural engineering may be for you. Architectural engineers need to be aesthetic as well as technical, creative as well as rational. They need to know if what looks good on paper is also technically possible.

Architectural engineers have four major areas of specialization or emphasis:

1. Structural Engineering - They consider the forces of hurricane winds, snow, or earthquakes in building design.
2. Mechanical Systems - Are concerned with regulating interior air flow; determining wall thickness; choosing materials; and designing interior and exterior heat sources, plumbing, heating, and air conditioning.

3. Electrical and lighting systems - Are responsible for distributing electricity throughout the building.

4. Construction Management - Are responsible for managing construction projects; they focus on safety, cost, and construction methods.

Currently, there are only seventeen accredited architectural engineering programs in the United States. Check out the Architectural Engineering Institute (AEI) of the American Society for Civil Engineering at www.aeinstitute.org for more information on this exciting branch of engineering.

AUTOMOTIVE ENGINEERING

MEDIAN STARTING SALARY (FOR MECHANICAL ENGINEERING): $58,600

MEDIAN INCOME (FOR MECHANICAL ENGINEERING): $84,770

Because of environmental concerns—increased fuel efficiency regulations and air-quality standards, this is a great time to become an automotive engineer. In fact, if motorized vehicles are your interest, there is no better career to pursue than engineering. There are more engineers in this industry than any other. Engineers are needed to design, test, evaluate the safety, and performance of every system within every type of vehicle. Electric cars, hybrids, and alternative fuel vehicles all have teams of engineers behind the engines, transmissions, suspensions, brakes, electrical systems, aerodynamics, and manufacturing processes. There is no part of any vehicle that isn't designed, tested, analyzed and evaluated by automotive engineers.

Automotive engineering is a branch of mechanical engineering. According to the U.S. Department of Labor, by the year 2018, there will be an extra 87,000 jobs for mechanical engineers and mechanical engineering is also listed as one of the top 50 occupations with the most openings that requires a bachelor's degree. Most students major in mechanical engineering with an emphasis in automotive engineering. Since mechanical engineering is such a broad discipline, select a school whose area of emphasis matches your own interests. For example, if you are interested in automotive engineering and wish to broaden your choice of schools, select a college that teaches mechanical engineering with an emphasis in automotive engineering such as the University of Illinois, Michigan, or Tennessee. If your primary interest is to make cars or any vehicle go faster, choose a school with an emphasis in combustion, materials, fluid mechanics, or thermodynamics. If electric cars are your interest, choose a school that specializes or has classes in battery technology.

Most automotive engineers are employed by the major automobile companies but they may also work for any companies that support transportation such as bus manufacturers, aviation companies, off road vehicle companies, motorcycle companies and the like. In the U.S. there are almost 10,000 companies that design and manufacture car parts and with new types of vehicles on the horizon, this number is expected to increase. From researching alternative fuels and aerodynamics to improve fuel efficiency to improving the suspensions of sports cars or electric buses, these engineers are leading the way to lower emissions and an improved environment.

Automotive engineers are involved in every aspect of vehicle design. Thanks to the competitiveness of the automotive industry, these engineers can expect a future of growth in an exciting and challenging environment. Car makers are clamoring for engineers to help them meet new governmental regulations and develop cars that an environmentally conscious public wants to purchase. Automotive engineers enjoy benefits such as experiencing cutting-edge technology first hand, being involved in several stages of new car development, and most likely receiving discounts on their own new vehicles.

Honda and Ford Motor Company both offer internship and co-op work experience for students interested in automotive engineering. Ford offers hands-on experience working full time during the summer and Honda offers year round internships, part-time jobs (2 days a week), and co-op programs.

Toyota employs 317,000 people worldwide and seeks graduates that have a B.S. in mechanical engineering, a general understanding of standard engineering theory, excellent problem solving techniques, an understanding and willingness to work on CAD, excellent communication and interpersonal skills to communicate effectively with suppliers, and experience in an automotive internship or co-op is preferred (good qualities for working for any transportation company).

According to the New York Times, GM, Ford, and Chrysler will need to hire thousands of engineers to meet the demand for cars that get 54.5 mpg by the year 2026 set by the Obama Administration. Car manufacturers understand that being green is not only good for the environment but it's also critical to being competitive worldwide. The public wants to purchase vehicles that are environmentally conscientious and the only way car manufacturers can stay in business is to provide these cars. The auto makers are currently working with colleges and universities to develop courses to train and retrain the engineers who will be expected to develop tomorrow's electric, hybrid and alternative fuel cars. Karl Stracke, GM's vice president of global vehicle engineering, said today's automotive engineers must be cross-trained in several different types of engineering.

Visit the Society of Automotive Engineers (SAE International) website at www.sae.org to get more information.

BIOMEDICAL ENGINEERING

MEDIAN STARTING SALARY: **$68,000**

MEDIAN INCOME: **$86,960**

Biomedical engineering is, in a very real sense, people engineering. The objective of biomedical engineering is to enhance health care by solving complex medical problems using engineering principles. Those who specialize in this field want to serve the public, work with health care professionals, and interact with living systems. This broad field allows a large choice of sub-specialties. Many students say they choose biomedical engineering because it is people-oriented.

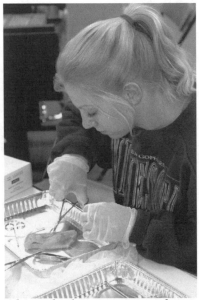

Imagine designing a medical device that appears to breath life into someone. The pacemaker was invented by biomedical engineers who literally gave recipients the ability to perform physical

A biomedical engineering student performing a dissection in a biology laboratory.

activities such as climbing a flight of stairs or walking around the block.

The biomedical engineering field changes rapidly. New technology is designed and fabricated every day. Biomedical engineers can expect a satisfying career with tremendous diversity and growth potential. The field includes many branches: biomechanical, bioelectrical, biochemical, rehabilitation, clinical, and genetic engineering. There are also many sub-specialties within biomedical engineering such as surgical lasers, telemedicine, nuclear medicine, and clinical computer systems.

Examples of specializations within biomedical engineering include:

- Artificial organs such as hearing aids, kidneys, hearts, blood oxygenators, synthetic blood vessels, pacemakers and joints.
- Prosthetic devices such as arms, legs, hands, feet, fingers, toes, and facial organs.
- Automated patient monitoring devices for surgery or intensive care. Automated monitoring devices also include monitoring healthy persons in unusual environments such as astronauts in space or deep sea divers.
- Blood chemistry sensors for detecting higher or lower levels of potassium, sodium, O_2, CO_2, and pH balance.
- Advanced therapeutic and surgical devices such as laser systems for eye surgery, endoscopic surgery, and automated delivery of insulin.
- Computer-based systems for diagnosing diseases and hospital management.
- Clinical laboratory design such as computer analyzers for blood or urine samples and cardiac catheterization laboratories.
- Medical imaging such as ultrasound, computer assisted tomography (CAT), magnetic resonance imaging (MRI), and positron emission tomography (PET) systems.
- Physiologic system computer modeling for blood pressure control, renal function, seeing and hearing nervous circuits, and more.
- Biomaterials design such as the mechanical, transport, and biocompatibility properties of implantable artificial organs, limbs, and materials.
- Biomechanical applications using gait analysis and growth factor applications.
- Sports medicine in rehabilitation and physical therapy as well as external support devices.

A fascinating application of biomechanical engineering, according to Ellen Morrissey and Donald Lehr of the Nolan/ Lehr Group, is the helmets for hockey players. Though they appear to be made of a single piece of material, they are actually three different parts fitted together in an intricate geometric configuration refined over the years for maximum energy absorption. (To test the helmet's ability to attenuate impacts, manufacturers fit helmets with instrumental test heads and then drop them several meters. At the end of the drop, known as a "sudden deceleration," the testers examine the helmet's level of protection and whether it has withstood impacts from 275 to 300 G-forces.) Besides providing protection, the helmet must also be light enough to keep the head cool, since hockey players are in constant motion and release a great deal of heat through their head. Lightness also allows players to accelerate at high speeds and then, since sudden stops square the effect of inertia, stop without tumbling off balance.

BIOCHEMICAL ENGINEERING—Biochemical engineers concern themselves with body responses on a microscopic level. These engineers study the interactions between artificial materials that may cause negative reactions in the human body. They apply anatomy, biochemistry, and cellular mechanics to understand diseases and modes of intervention. They developed woven acrylic artificial arteries to prevent blood clotting in artificial blood vessels. And they designed and constructed the artificial kidney for patients with incurable kidney disease.

BIOELECTRICAL ENGINEERING—Biomedical engineering with an electrical emphasis is a popular choice among students. Bioelectrical inventions are everywhere, from digital ear thermometers to sophisticated MRI machines. Another bioelectrical development is the pacemaker, a device that senses irregular or arrested heart rhythms and restores the rhythms by giving electrical stimulation to the heart muscle. Bioelectrical engineers have also developed the electrocardiogram machine, which records, through electrodes placed on the skin, the beating of a heart. Bioelectrical engineers may design software or devices to aid doctors and hospitals such as electrophysiology cardiac monitors or telemedicine equipment. They may design devices to allow patients to self-monitor their conditions, or they may help a paraplegic become self-sufficient by designing an electrical system to regulate all switches and/ or appliances in the patient's house.

BIOMECHANICAL ENGINEERING—Biomechanical engineering or biomechanics is the specialty that sees the human body as a mechanical structure. These specialists investigate the motion of the human body, the stresses on bones and muscles, and the deformation of artificial materials, such as bones and joints. They might work for a company such as Nike to design a new running shoe after studying the impact caused by running. Biomechanical engineers may also design artificial limbs, joint replacements, or new materials to replace ligaments, tendons, or bones. An early development from a biomechanical engineer was the invention of the iron lung, which was an airtight respirator consisting of a metal tank that enclosed the entire body except for the head. It provided artificial respiration by contracting and expanding the walls of the chest.

CLINICAL ENGINEERING—Clinical engineering is the branch of biomedical engineering that applies technology to health care in organizations such as hospitals and long-term care facilities, and for medical equipment vendors. Clinical engineers must understand the relationship of the equipment to the diagnosis, care, and treatment of the patient. High-risk assessments and the development of maintenance schedules and protocols are some of the other tasks they perform. They may also provide training for doctors, nurses, and other health professionals on the effective use of all medical equipment, and they may maintain the equipment. Clinical engineers may also evaluate equipment prior to purchase, test the equipment for safety, or modify existing hospital equipment. In addition, they may participate in accident or incident investigations.

GENETIC, CELLULAR AND TISSUE ENGINEERING—Genetic, Cellular, and Tissue engineering is a new branch of biomedical engineering that researches ways to harness biomedical problems on a microscopic level. Researchers manipulate DNA, stimulate or retard cellular growth, and study the structure and mechanics of cells to better understand disease and detect methods of intervention. Genetic and agricultural engineers also design products to break down oil slicks efficiently.

REHABILITATION ENGINEERING—Rehabilitation engineering is another popular specialty within biomedical engineering. Rehabilitation engineers participate in the research and development of technology to assist people with disabilities. According to the Biomedical Engineering Society, "Rehabilitation engineers enhance the capabilities and improve the quality of life for individuals with physical and cognitive impairments."

Assistive technology includes devices such as powered wheelchairs, talking computers, hearing aids, electronic talking devices, and any facilities that are modified, including grab bars for showers and restrooms. Recreational assistive technology such as specially adapted skis and fishing poles are also available. If rehabilitation engineering interests you, watch the Special Olympics to see the assortment of assistive technology devices available. Imagine the feeling of power and accomplishment associated with giving a disabled person a new lease on life, providing a way to meet everyday life challenges successfully, and eliminating some of the challenges associated with having a disability in today's society.

A rehabilitation engineer may work on site with a person recently confined to a wheelchair to redesign the person's work space; changes might include a desk that can be raised and lowered at the push of a button, wider doorways, and indoor ramps. A rehabilitation engineer may also redesign computer systems to assist people with cognitive or physical disabilities. One rehabilitation engineer designed a Braille keyboard so blind people can type; another developed a system that enables people that are paralyzed below the waist to drive an automobile.

As you can see, the diverse field of biomedical engineering offers a real way to make a large impact on society. Biomedical engineers work in hospitals, government regulatory agencies, corporations, medical device companies, research labs, and universities. Many go to medical school; biomedical engineers have a higher acceptance rate into medical school than people with any other degree. Many go to law school and become regulatory requirement attorneys for the Federal Drug Administration (FDA). Some go into teaching, and many become consultants or advisers to medical companies.

The Biomedical Engineering Society (BMES) has an excellent website at www.bmes.org that details the numerous specialties available within the field and provides links for additional information resources such as job opportunities, individual state BMES chapters, and prominent companies in the medical industry.

BIOMEDICAL ENGINEERING TECHNOLOGY

AVERAGE STARTING SALARY
BACHELOR'S DEGREE IN BIOMEDICAL ENGINEERING TECHNOLOGY IS $35,000
ASSOCIATE'S DEGREE IN BIOMEDICAL ENGINEERING TECHNOLOGY IS $30,000

Imagine being a biomedical technologist or technician (BMET) for a large hospital. All day, patients are admitted or diagnosed by hospital staff. The majority of the time, a diagnosis is made by using some type of electronic equipment. From simply the act of taking a patient's temperature using a digital thermometer to assessing arrhythmias using a cardiac monitor, biomedical engineering technologists and technicians are responsible for medical technology that enhances health care. BMETs are on the front line of health care, providing installation, design, manufacturing, training of hospital staff and personnel, and preventive maintenance for vital medical equipment. The work of the BMET ensures that all health care professionals can provide the care and treatment that patients need.

Biomedical engineering technologists and technicians focus primarily on medical equipment for hospitals and medical service providers. These positions require that the BMET work closely with physicians, nurses, therapists, hospital staff and other technical professionals to understand, assess, and make certain the diagnostic and therapeutic equipment and life-saving devices are operating within specifications. This field is similar to clinical engineering, and some BMET graduates will even be called clinical engineers. The difference is that clinical engineers, with a bachelor's degree in biomedical engineering, may be more involved in design, modification, and pre-purchase assessments whereas the BMETs may be more application-oriented and involved in installing, modifying, inspecting, testing, calibrating, or repairing the equipment. In addition, a BMET might be more likely to work in a hospital or clinical setting, while a BME would more usually work at a company.

BMETs must be also quick thinkers. If any equipment breaks down in the middle of a procedure and the patient's life is held in the balance, the BMET will be called in "STAT" to fix the problem. They may find themselves running through hospital corridors as precious minutes are ticking. Problems that arise could be as simple as a circuit breaker tripping in the operating room to a kidney dialysis machine malfunctioning in the middle of treatment. Whatever the case, this career requires fast thinking and good problem solving skills.

Currently, there are only a few ABET accredited biomedical engineering technology programs in the United States. However, many schools offer programs in electronic engineering technology with an emphasis in medical instrumentation, devices, or environments.

There are three choices for majoring in biomedical engineering technology or biomedical engineering. The table below gives a basic understanding of the differences but both sections on biomedical engineering and biomedical engineering technology should be read to gain a more thorough understanding of the fields and the differences between them.

Degree Program	Degree Type	Primary Focus	Types of employers
Biomedical Engineering Technology (BMET)	Associate's Degree (technician)	Repair and maintain medical equipment, devices and technology in patient care. Train hospital staff on use of medical equipment.	Hospitals, medical equipment manufacturers
Biomedical Engineering Technology (BMET)	Bachelor's Degree (engineering technologist)	Manage and support the design, manufacture and use of medical equipment, devices and technology in patient care. Train hospital staff on use of medical equipment.	Hospitals, medical equipment manufacturers, leading edge companies for medical devices, sports equipment, nanotechnology, pharmaceuticals, prosthetics
Biomedical Engineering (BME)	Bachelor's Degree (engineer)	Investigate complex medical problems and develop engineering methods to solve them.	Over half of grads continue education (grad school or medical/dental school), staff engineer in a medical research laboratory, leading edge companies for medical devices, sports equipment, nanotechnology, pharmaceuticals, prosthetics

Degree comparison table of biomedical engineering and biomedical engineering technology.

Examples of Biomedical Engineering and Biomedical Engineering Technology in Sports:

- May design systems for motion analysis and biomechanical analysis of injuries or stress patterns for athletic shoe design
- May design systems to analyze the human body while skiing or snowboarding to aid in injury prevention
- May research the motion of many sports to determine the requirements for product design and keeping people safe
- May design new suits or model a swimmers performance on computer systems to analyze stroke capabilities
- May design systems to analyze the human body wearing a helmet for neck and spine injury prevention
- May research the impact aspects of many sports to determine the padding requirements

CERAMIC ENGINEERING

MEDIAN STARTING SALARY (FOR MATERIALS ENGINEERING): $62,000
MEDIAN INCOME (FOR MATERIALS ENGINEERING): $87,490

Computer chips, fiber optics, joint replacements, CDs, DVDs, VCRs, video games, watches, snow skis, phone lines, space shuttle tiles, safety glass windshields, dental restoration, bone implants, medical electronic equipment, airbag sensors, spark plugs, piston rings, bricks, cement, missiles, capacitors, resistors, electronic components, TV components, magnets, laser communications, lab equipment, bathroom sinks, kitchen appliances – all these and more depend on ceramics and the advances of the ceramic engineer.

Ceramic engineering could be called the smooth operator of the engineering world. It is almost impossible to avoid the advance of ceramics in your daily life. We rarely hear about the work of ceramic engineers or think about the everyday household items and electronic components that are possible only because of highly complex ceramic materials and processes.

Typically, as we grow up, we see ceramics in pottery class or think of ceramics as cereal bowls or plates. We might see ceramic tiles lining the interior of tunnels we drive through, reflecting any available light and making the tunnel easy to clean. Or we might think of ceramic tile as something to walk on in the bathroom or kitchen. There are many more applications for ceramics and opportunities for ceramic engineers. Ceramics is a cutting-edge, low-cost material with unique properties that make it a dream come true for scientists and engineers.

The space shuttle is a wonderful example of a cutting-edge, high-temperature ceramic application. The entire shuttle is covered with ceramic tiles that protect the aluminum shell.

The tiles can withstand temperatures of 1400° Celsius (C) that are prevalent at the nose of the shuttle as it exits or enters the atmosphere. If the tiles were not present, the aluminum shell would melt at 660° C. There could be no moon landing, no space study without ceramic materials.

Ceramic engineers look for different uses for ceramics, create new ceramic products, and design processes for making ceramics. They take raw materials such as clay and sand and convert them into usable, useful products. They use the periodic table to combine different elements that create new materials for specific applications such as increasing or decreasing the electrical, magnetic, or thermal properties. Ceramic engineering combines physics, chemistry, and materials.

The Ceramic Engineering Department at the Missouri University of Science and Technology at Rolla explains that ceramic engineers may:

- Develop improved heat tiles to protect the space shuttle and the future supersonic space plane from the searing heat of reentry into the earth's atmosphere.
- Produce ceramic teeth, bones, and joints to replace parts of the human body or improve advanced medical

equipment to continue research in the war against disease.
- Help make innovative, ultra-fast computer systems using ceramic superconductors, lasers, and glass optical fibers.
- Develop materials to enclose and support aircraft engines that run at high temperatures.
- Improve fiber optic cables that allow doctors to see inside the human body and permit the human voice to travel thousands of miles under the ocean without distortion.
- Discover new ways to use ceramics to build highways and bridges, or to carry water and waste to treatment plants.

If ceramic engineering sounds like the career for you, visit the websites of all of the colleges that offer ceramic engineering, and take a tour of materials engineering departments in your area. The American Ceramic Society/The National Institute of Ceramic Engineers have a great website with helpful information such as links to all of the accredited ceramic engineering programs, co-op opportunities, internships, and ceramic news. Student competitions involve contests such as the ceramic putting competition in which students design putters and golf balls made of ceramic; mug contests in which ceramic mugs are judged on strength, insulation, and artistic merit; and a speaking competition. Visit www.acers.org for more information about the opportunities and challenges of a career in ceramic engineering.

CHEMICAL ENGINEERING
MEDIAN STARTING SALARY: $65,403
MEDIAN INCOME: $94,350

As creative and innovative problem solvers, chemical engineers enjoy great diversity in their intellectually challenging field. Chemical engineering offers one of the highest starting salaries of all the engineering disciplines. Everything that our senses enjoy consists of chemicals in one way or another. Chemical engineers have worked on creating the purple rose that has no thorns, the caramel on a caramel apple, and even your tennis shoes. The chemical engineering profession has improved water and waste systems, created new drugs and drug delivery systems, and improved the gas mileage of most transportation. Most chemical engineers work in manufacturing, pharmaceuticals, healthcare, design and construction, pulp and paper, petrochemicals, sports equipment design, food processing, specialty chemicals, microelectronics, electronic and advanced materials, polymers, business services, biotechnology, and the environmental health and safety industries.

Chemical engineers can choose from many specialties within the discipline. A chemical engineering student who picks a track in environmental engineering might be interested in reducing pollution or  producing better food. Chemical engineers who focus on biomedical engineering are often called biochemical engineers; they may design new or improved artificial organs or they may work in the pharmaceutical industry. An athletic chemical engineer may be interested in working for a sporting goods company designing better rubber soles for basketball shoes. If you are more attracted to the big picture, you might see yourself looking for ways to streamline processes or increase safety with a specialty as a process design engineer.

Traditionally, chemical, petroleum, and pharmaceutical companies employed the bulk of the chemical engineering profession. Pharmaceutical companies still employ a large number of chemical engineers to research, develop, or design their product lines. Now, however, many chemical engineers work in biotechnology, material science (such as the plastics, rubber, ceramics, and metals industries), and electronics. The food industry, the Department of Energy, and the Environmental Protection Agency have also become prominent employers of chemical engineers.

Many chemicals engineers have opted for careers in research. A chemical engineer who goes to medical school could become a medical doctor specializing in rare diseases or a medical researcher. A chemical engineer who goes to law school could be a patent attorney or a specialized attorney for a company that has invented a new drug or drug delivery system.

The American Institute of Chemical Engineers (AIChE) offers a student chapter to help students step gracefully into the real world of chemical engineering. Thousands of students across the nation participate in the organization at more than 150 campus locations. The organization supports students and encourages growth by offering numerous scholarships, competitions, and awards. Visit their website www.aiche.org and see for yourself all the benefits you can gain by joining this society. The site is packed with information, has profiles of what many chemical engineers do on a daily basis, and gives realistic career information.

CIVIL ENGINEERING

MEDIAN STARTING SALARY: $51,793

MEDIAN INCOME: $79,340

Civil engineers are changing the world! Civil engineering is one of the oldest, largest and most amazing branches of engineering. Traditionally, civil engineers planned and designed such things as roads, bridges, high-rises, dams, and airports. However, over time, civil engineering has evolved to encompass much more. If you want to solve the energy crisis, clean up the environment, or be a part of a world that helps people have access to healthy food, clean water, and a stable infrastructure, you should seriously consider civil engineering. Civil engineering is closely connected to the environment, both natural

and human-made. As our current understanding of technology increases, demand for the diverse talents of civil engineers will increase too.

Civil engineers are currently involved in a large variety of "green" projects such as:

- Designing green buildings that have the capability to power themselves with various forms of green energy.
- Constructing anything needed for installing any type of alternative energy - solar panels, wind turbines, geothermal heat pumps, hydropower facilities, etc.
- Designing the offshore wind turbine structures that are embedded in the ocean floor that can withstand the weight of ice and the impact of waves and hurricane winds. They may be responsible for mooring systems and running electrical cable underwater.
- Making sure we always have access to clean drinking water.
- Studying air pollution and finding ways to improve it.
- Designing and directing the construction of dams to prevent flooding, improve irrigation, provide a water supply, and generate hydroelectric power.
- Building more fuel efficient ships to ensure that it can withstand the weight of cargo and the impact of waves. Combat ships must be able to withstand battle damage from weapons such as missiles, torpedoes, and underwater mines.

Civil engineers enjoy being able to choose from many specialties within their discipline, such as environmental, transportation, structural, geotechnical, or water/wastewater management.

- As an environmental engineer they may monitor air pollution and discover new ways to obtain clean drinking water. According to the American Society of Civil Engineers (ASCE), "The skills of environmental engineers are becoming increasingly important as we attempt to protect the fragile resources of our planet. Environmental engineers translate physical, chemical, and biological processes into systems to destroy toxic substances, remove pollutants from water, reduce nonhazardous solid waste volumes, eliminate contaminants from the air, and develop groundwater supplies. In this field, you might be called upon to resolve problems of providing safe drinking water, cleaning up sites contaminated with hazardous materials, cleaning up and preventing air pollution, treating wastewater, and managing solid wastes."

- As a geotechnical engineer they may help maintain the Hoover dam or construct embankments, seawalls and levee systems. Geotechnical engineers may also be involved in running pipelines under the Atlantic ocean, building tunnels, and anything else that involves creating infrastructure on, in, or with earth.
- As a structural engineer they might work to make buildings or roads earthquake, hurricane, tsunami or flood safe. The structural engineer may also design offshore oil rigs, roller coasters, bridges or even a coliseum that hosts sporting events and concerts. Structural engineers must have an excellent understanding of material properties to know what to expect if something is built with plastic vs. steel vs. wood, etc.
- As a transportation engineer they will design the transportation of the future. These engineers are also known as people and product movers. That may include working with air vehicles, such as helicopters or airplanes, or it may mean working with water vehicles, such as new types of boats that can move product across the ocean more quickly or efficiently. In addition, transportation engineers could work on land vehicles, such as cars or high-speed trains that will either move products across the country or improve public transportation.
- As a construction engineer they might build any new building or construction project. Construction engineers typically manage construction projects and are involved in the budget, materials, planning, and equipment.

There is no limit to the versatility and opportunity of the civil engineering profession. Reed Brockman, a civil engineer for AECOM in Boston said, "My special interest is in bridge inspection and rehabilitation. I look at each bridge as if it were a patient – a big patient. Some patients look healthy when you first visit them, but turn out to have something wrong, while some others that look beat up are in generally good health. Either way, I take pride in knowing what symptoms to expect, and what should be done to get the bridges back into shape. Actually, there's a

Reed Brockman - Civil Engineer for AECOM in Boston, MA

great many other things I enjoy about my work: getting outdoors, climbing, constantly using my communication skills, and solving the puzzle of accessing some of the more complicated structures (renting cranes, barges, snooper trucks, etc.). I equally enjoy designing bridges and tunnels, especially coordinating the many different aspects into one design: the needs of the neighbors, maintaining overhead clearances, making sure rainwater can find its way off the roadway, giving all the pipes and cable ducts a home, and, of course, making it strong, easily maintained, and beautiful."

Some civil engineers opt for a career in research, where they may attempt to find stronger, and more resilient materials. A civil engineer who goes to law school could be an earthquake or hurricane insurance attorney, or simply a specialized attorney for a major construction company. A civil engineer who gets an MBA could open their own consulting firm or they could work on the bid processes of negotiating bridge, building, shopping mall, or amusement park projects.

The ASCE supports students and encourages growth by offering numerous scholarships, competitions, and awards to its student members. The ASCE also sponsors competitions such as the Concrete Canoe, and students in this society can get involved in projects such as Habitat for Humanity. Their website (www.asce. org) includes a listing of internships, colleges, and universities that teach civil engineering and civil engineering technology, profiles of civil engineers, and other career resources. Other items of interest include a database of job postings, student chapter links, event calendars, membership contests, membership forms, discussion forums dedicated to topics that affect civil engineering students, and much more.

For more information about civil engineering and preparing to work as a civil engineer, pick up a copy of *From Sundaes to Space Stations: Careers in Civil Engineering* at engineeringedu.com.

CIVIL OR CONSTRUCTION ENGINEERING TECHNOLOGY

THE AVERAGE STARTING SALARY FOR A GRADUATE WITH:
BACHELOR'S DEGREE IN CIVIL ENGINEERING TECHNOLOGY IS $35,550
ASSOCIATE'S DEGREE IN CIVIL ENGINEERING TECHNOLOGY IS $28,000

Civil or construction engineering technologists and technicians generate the drawings and specifications to create buildings, parks, structures, bridges, roads, water systems, tunnels, seawalls, embankments, etc. Technologists can design the structures and also work on designs developed by an engineer. Technologists can work independently but technicians normally work directly under the supervision of an engineer or technologist. All are involved in the various stages of design, documentation and construction. They work for consulting firms, wastewater treatment plants, federal, state, or local government agencies (such as a department of transportation), material testing laboratories, construction contracting firms, architectural firms, utility companies, manufacturing companies, and similar companies. Technicians work for the same types of companies and may perform drafting and/or surveying support or be involved in the installation and maintenance of the same structures, machines, and water systems. It is an exciting field rich in opportunities not only locally and nationally but also globally.

Technologists and technicians may find themselves in all stages of planning, designing, drafting, surveying, and analyzing such things as where water flows after a rain (drainage), watersheds, pipelines, waterways, roads, bridges, dams, water treatment facilities and/or any other infrastructure. This means a lot of the work is done outdoors, in many different settings. They also inspect buildings and structures, install or operate water pumps, run tests on soil and river water in laboratories, write reports, communicate with other members on the team, and give presentations about their findings. A technologist who works as a construction inspector could make sure that contractors  follow specifications, proposals, and state guidelines. A technologist working for the Department of Transportation could make adjustments to the plans, specifications and estimates on bridge, culvert, and road projects. A technician who works for a civil engineering firm could be on the team that helps oversee the rehabilitation of a road or installs new drainage, curbs, sidewalks, and lighting. Many states require (Professional Engineer) PE registration for many of these activities such as planning, designing, surveying, and making changes to the plans. Civil engineering technologists are excellent candidates to become licensed surveyors. The testing to become licensed is similar to becoming a PE.

There are three choices for majoring in civil engineering technology and civil engineering. The table below gives a basic understanding of the differences but both sections on civil engineering and civil engineering technology should be read to gain a more thorough understanding of the fields and the differences between them.

Degree Program	Degree Type	Primary Focus	Types of employers
Civil Engineering Technology	Associate's Degree (technician)	Drafting, surveying, inspecting, operating and installing equipment. Will work on a team under the supervision of a technologist or engineer. Cannot be licensed as a PE.	Consulting firms, wastewater treatment plants, federal, state, or local government agencies, material testing laboratories, construction contracting firms, architectural firms, utility companies, manufacturing companies, and similar companies
Civil Engineering Technology	Bachelor's Degree (engineering technologist)	Construction inspecting, soil testing, design, planning, documentation, analysis and testing.	
Civil Engineering	Bachelor's Degree (engineer)	Investigate complex environmental, geological, structural and transportation problems and develop engineering methods to solve them.	

Degree comparison table of civil engineering and civil or construction engineering technology.

COMPUTER ENGINEERING

MEDIAN STARTING SALARY: $56,201
MEDIAN INCOME: $100,920

Computer engineering is one of the fastest growing and most interesting fields you can pursue. It is very similar to electrical engineering, except that computer engineers work exclusively with computers and computer systems or equipment. The computer revolution has created countless jobs in every field of technology. Computer engineers, computer engineering technologists, computer scientists, and information technologists are all in high demand.

Computer engineers can work in hardware or software but for the purposes of this guide, computer engineers are those that work on the hardware side and develop hardware technologies, such as computer architecture, and those that link the computers together, such as networks and systems. Software engineers work on the software side. They deal with applications, such as artificial intelligence, and operating systems that run computers and related systems.

Computer engineering deals with the many aspects of computer systems and it is full of exciting and diverse opportunities. Information technology has created a plethora of job opportunities for the talented and highly skilled computer engineer. These engineers may research, design, develop, test manufacture, or install computer systems, networks,  circuit boards, integrated circuits (computer chips), operating systems, software or peripheral equipment such as keyboards, mice, printers, speakers, or microphones. They may also plan computer layouts, or research future applications or environments for computers. For example, computers are in automobiles, microwaves, iPods, watches, cell phones, mobile devices, video games, and much more. Some computer engineers may be at work right now trying to figure out how to embed computers into shoes that will grow more spring if you are walking or running quickly, prescription eye glasses that can eliminate bi- or trifocals by detecting eye strain, or ovens that can double as freezers and be programmed to turn on, defrost, and then cook your dinner.

Many computer engineers work for large corporations, helping employees with hardware or software problems. They may create, maintain, or install local-area networks (LANs), parallel architecture, multiprocessor architecture, real-time systems, or multimedia within companies.

According to the IEEE computer society, "Computing professionals might find themselves in a variety of environments in academia, research, industry, government, private and business organizations -- analyzing problems for solutions, formulating and testing, using advanced communications or multi-media equipment, or working in teams for product development. Here's a short list of research and vocational areas in computing.

- Artificial Intelligence -- Develop computers that simulate human learning and reasoning ability.
- Computer Design and Engineering -- Design new computer circuits, microchips, and other electronic components.
- Computer Architecture -- Design new computer instruction sets, and combine electronic or optical components to provide powerful but cost-effective computing.
- Information Technology -- Develop and manage information systems that support a business or organization.
- Software Engineering -- Develop methods for the production of software systems on time, within budget, and with few or no defects.
- Computer Theory -- Investigate the fundamental theories of how computers solve problems, and apply the results to other areas of computer science.

- Operating Systems and Networks -- Develop the basic software computers use to supervise themselves or to communicate with other computers.
- Software Applications -- Apply computing and technology to solving problems outside the computer field -- in education or medicine, for example."

Computer engineers often work as part of a team that designs new hardware, software, and systems. A core team may be composed of engineering, marketing, manufacturing, and design people who work together until the product is released. Computer engineers may also work in research and development. To get talking computers, voice-activated automobiles or appliances, and other inventions affordable and to market, someone needs to research and develop them. For more information visit the IEEE Computer Society at www.computer.org.

COMPUTER ENGINEERING TECHNOLOGY
THE AVERAGE STARTING SALARY FOR A GRADUATE WITH:
BACHELOR'S DEGREE IN COMPUTER ENGINEERING TECHNOLOGY IS
$35,000 - $45,000
ASSOCIATE'S DEGREE IN COMPUTER ENGINEERING TECHNOLOGY IS
$25,000 - $35,000

Computer engineering technologists and technicians are often considered modern day heroes. They may focus on hardware or software issues. When computer users can't figure out how to install or maintain their computers or systems, the technician is called to save the day. When companies need custom applications and network systems designed, they call the computer engineering technologist. In this age of heavy computer usage, with companies using computers for a large variety of functions, the computer engineering technologists and technician are invaluable in keeping equipment running, updating software, maintaining connectivity, and interfacing with users.

These unsung heroes typically work for large companies, installing, testing, operating, and maintaining the internal systems. They may also find employment with companies that sell computers, such as Fry's, Best Buy, and Office Depot; at computer repair shops; or at independent emergency repair facilities. Other common work locations include computer and peripheral manufacturing facilities, computer distribution facilities, computer research facilities and educational institutions.

Technicians in this field may find themselves making house calls to help restore a computer that was plagued by a virus, troubleshooting printing problems, or helping with software applications. If the technician works for a distributor, they may give tech support on the telephone and build customer systems in a laboratory. The career paths in this field are varied, flexible, and abundant.

The exact job and responsibilities of a technologist vs. a technician depend on the amount of education, the experience and the employer. In general, the technologist with a bachelor's degree will have more responsibility and may be in charge of transforming a concept into a prototype or product. They may have to look at design specifications and know what materials are available to bring the idea to reality. A technician with an associate's degree may take that prototype or product from the technologist and run tests on it to confirm the specifications and ensure the design is working as intended. However, in this field, experience plays a far greater role in defining job description and responsibilities than educational paperwork.

There are three choices for majoring in computer engineering technology or computer engineering. The table below gives a basic understanding of the differences but both sections on computer engineering and computer engineering technology should be read to gain a more thorough understanding of the fields and the differences between them.

Degree Program	Degree Type	Primary Focus	Types of employers
Computer Engineering Technology	Associate's Degree (technician)	Aid in developing prototypes; build, install, repair and maintain computer software, hardware and peripherals.	Retail outlets, computer repair shops and independent emergency repair facilities
Computer Engineering Technology	Bachelor's Degree (engineering technologist)	Manage and support the design, manufacture and use of computer equipment, devices, peripherals and associated technology.	Computer and peripheral manufacturing facilities, computer distribution facilities, computer research facilities and educational institutions.
Computer Engineering	Bachelor's Degree (engineer)	Investigate complex computer and network problems and develop engineering methods to solve them.	Computer software and hardware design companies. Computer and peripheral manufacturing facilities, computer distribution facilities, computer research facilities and educational institutions.

Degree comparison table of computer engineering and computer engineering technology.

ELECTRICAL ENGINEERING

MEDIAN STARTING SALARY: $57,600
MEDIAN INCOME: $89,630

The diverse and progressive field of electrical and electronic engineering has grown rapidly and is one of the largest branches of engineering. Electrical engineers (EEs) are imaginative problem solvers. They enjoy challenges.

According to the Institute of Electrical and Electronic Engineering (IEEE), "Electrical engineering is about 100 years old, and electronics has been a science for about 75 years. Electrical engineers specializing in power work with motors and generators, and design transmission lines and power plants. EEs specializing in electronics deal with communications, such as radio, television, and cell phones, and with digital and analog circuit technologies. All engineers draw from the fundamentals of science and mathematics. They design and work with electrical, electronic, electro-optical, and electromechanical devices, circuits, and systems. They collaborate with other professionals in developing sophisticated software tools that support design, verification, and testing. Electrical engineering is a discipline that integrates many other disciplines, such as physics, chemistry, mathematics, computer software and hardware, solid-state electronics, communications, electromagnetics and optics, signals and signal processing, systems science, reliability, engineering economics, and manufacturing."

The developments of electrical and electronic engineers are everywhere. There are thousands of electrical devices and systems available today that electrical engineers have somehow touched. Anything you plug into the wall – stereos, computers, microwaves, televisions, power tools, air-conditioners, and major appliances – has been touched by an electrical engineer. Even things you can't plug into the wall – satellites, cellular phones, and beepers – have been designed, manufactured, or modified by electrical engineers.

Major specializations within electrical engineering include power plant/energy, communications, optical engineering, and computer engineering. Electrical engineers who specialize in power applications may work for utility companies designing power distribution systems. Or they may work on generating electricity by using alternative energy sources.

Engineers in this area may also decide they want to be a part of the "green economy" and get a job working in renewable energy. In this capacity they may develop the technology to generate, store, or distribute the renewable solar energy harvested from solar panels. They may be responsible for grid connections, designing the transmission lines or the logistics of transporting energy across the land. Or, they may design electrical, computer and automation systems, alarms, and communication systems.

According to the IEEE, "the key to employability is acquiring the knowledge and skill sets in demand by employers. Those who fail to gain or maintain knowledge and skill with tools, such as computer-aided design (CAD) and other software relevant to their work, are disadvantaged. The lack of communication and interpersonal skills, needed to work effectively on teams, can also be a stumbling block."

The IEEE has a fantastic website at www.ieee.org that is jam-packed with information about the world of electrical engineering. See the numerous divisions within the world's largest technical professional society. The website has pages on internships and scholarships. It lists information on job hunting and has a job bank. Twenty-five percent of the world's technical papers are produced each year through the IEEE. The institute has student chapters at numerous universities and offers student benefits such as group insurance programs, credit cards, auto and education loans, Kinko's copy service discounts, and car rental discounts. Students receive the IEEE SPECTRUM magazine and a discount on membership. The website is well worth the time invested in browsing.

FEATURE ARTICLE

THE FOOTSTEPS OF AN ELECTRICAL ENGINEER - IVAR SANDERS, ELECTRONIC PRODUCT DEVELOPER AND INVENTOR OF THE NOKIA WIRELESS ROUTER

You would think, after spending my days designing wireless routers, a new type of product that gives families high-speed access to the Internet using microwave radios, that I would have had my fill of technology. But no, I love technology, and spend at least some part of my spare time improving our home network or home multimedia distribution or just tinkering with a new technology just to see how it works. Unlike the left-brain vision some folks have of engineers, I view myself as a kind of artist with a practical twist, using a special set of tools to create new types of devices that help people or are just plain fun.

I would never have guessed that, as a sixth-grader, my fascination with the ham radio equipment being used by my buddy's father would eventually lead to such a satisfying and creative career, but, in hindsight, it certainly created the spark. I had to know how to create devices that allowed people to talk to each other over great distances with nothing between them except open space! How was this possible? It seemed intimidating at first, but I had not yet learned how to manipulate the tools of this particular trade, nor even what the tools were. The spark had been ignited though, and like most things that seem difficult at first, when learned a step at a time, it eventually made sense.

Then I had a chance to put the knowledge to use. Starting in the aerospace industry, I had the opportunity to see the results of my work used in interesting ways, including Space Shuttle navigation displays, and automation of the National Weather Service. The biggest personal joy has, however, come from creating products used by everyday people to improve their lives.

Seeing a product I have designed receive a favorable review in a consumer magazine is a great ego boost, but nothing compares to watching a stranger pull a product I have designed from a store shelf, buy it, and take it home to be enjoyed. I recall being in a large electronics retail store a few years ago. I noticed two people, who were apparently strangers to each other, discussing which of several similar products on the self to buy. They offered each other their own particular needs for the product, and compared the features. Much to my delight, they ended up buying my product! What a great feeling! I wanted to go up to them, say thanks, and tell them that they had chosen a product I had designed, but decided it would be better to be quiet and keep the pride and joy to myself. You see, unlike painters or sculptors who get to sign their creative works, engineers have often not received such public recognition (although, as the public gains a better understanding of what engineers do and their place in the product creation process, this may be changing). Nevertheless, even though I enjoy technology for its own sake, the incident certainly gave me some nice strokes that wiped out whatever frustration there may have been while learning to be an engineer or while designing that product!

Now, more than 40 years after that first youngster's view into the world of possibilities created by ham radio, after the formal training of an engineering degree, and after many years of combining a knowledge and fascination of technology to create products that everyday people find useful in their lives, I can't think of a more satisfying career.

ELECTRONIC / ELECTRICAL ENGINEERING TECHNOLOGY
THE AVERAGE STARTING SALARY FOR A GRADUATE WITH:
BACHELOR'S DEGREE IN ELECTRONIC ENGINEERING TECHNOLOGY IS
$35,000 - $45,000
ASSOCIATE'S DEGREE IN ELECTRONIC ENGINEERING TECHNOLOGY IS
$25,000 - $35,000

Electronic engineering technologists design, develop, and manufacture everything that you plug into the wall - televisions, computers, refrigerators, microwaves, stereos, etc. They design, develop, work on and work with the electronic components that are in every device that runs on electricity. They are into electronic equipment, such as communication equipment; radar, industrial, wireless and medical monitoring or control devices; navigational equipment; and computers. They also manage and support cars that today have many electronic components: GPS, phones, Internet, electronic devices that allow the car to park without the intervention of the driver and the navigational systems that allow you to verbally tell the car to go to a specific place and the car will drive for you.

Electrical engineering technologists apply their skills to the generation and transmission of electricity. Many electrical engineering technologists work in green energy for solar panel, wind turbine, wave energy and geothermal design companies.

Electronic engineering technicians repair and maintaining electronic equipment used by businesses or individuals. They may work in product evaluation and testing, using measuring and diagnostic devices such as oscilloscopes, computer software and multimeters to adjust, test, and repair equipment.

Electronics have revolutionized the world. Everything from iPods, to cell phones, to GPS systems contain electronic components. Every business from the small shop owner, to utility companies, to federal government agencies, need technologists and technicians. The opportunities are far-reaching and abundant. So often, the engineering technologist or technician can save the day by helping companies run smoother and more efficiently.

- The small shop owner and large companies may not have a technician on staff, but when a machine breaks down, they call a field technician to fix the problem. The field technician may be responsible for installing and ensuring the normal operation of machines located within several companies in a certain geographic area. When equipment breaks down, the technician will first check for common causes of trouble, such as loose connections or obviously defective components. If routine checks do not locate the trouble, the technician may refer to schematics or repair manuals that show connections and provide instructions on how to locate problems. Many technicians will use software programs, multimeters, oscilloscopes, spectrum analyzers and signal generators in their diagnoses. If a machine cannot be repaired on-site, the field technician will arrange to transport the machine to a facility or repair shop where a bench technician can repair it. Some equipment may give an alarm if failing and other equipment may just break. The technician will likely be working on equipment from different technological era's.

- Alternative energy companies may hire technologists to design, develop or manufacture equipment for wind turbines and farms, solar panels and car recharging stations, or equipment to harvest and transmit energy from dams or other sources of electricity.

- Utility companies will hire engineering technologist as plant or electrical system operators. They most often hire technicians to do everything from installing, operating, maintaining, and controlling electric substations, to monitoring equipment and electric transformers that distribute electricity to homes and businesses.

- Federal government agencies hire technologists and technicians to maintain national security equipment, air traffic control systems, U.S. postal facilities, equipment in customs offices, the U.S. Mint, the Federal Reserve, the White House, and NASA space centers.

There are three choices for majoring in electronic/electrical engineering technology or electrical engineering. The table below gives a basic understanding of the differences but both sections on electrical engineering and electronic/electrical engineering technology should be read to gain a more thorough understanding of the fields and the differences between them.

Degree Program	Degree Type	Primary Focus	Types of employers
Electronic/ Electrical Engineering Technology (EET)	Associate's Degree (technician)	Install, build, repair and maintain electronic equipment, devices and technology. Train consumers on use of electrical equipment. Cannot be licensed as a PE.	Numerous industries hire these technicians. Jobs are available in small and large companies, manufacturing, distribution, government, education, and more.
Electronic/ Electrical Engineering Technology (EET)	Bachelor's Degree (engineering technologist)	Manage and support or modify the design, manufacture and use of electrical and electronic equipment, devices and technology. Make recommendations for improvements and oversee the work of engineering technicians	Utility companies, government agencies, alternative energy companies, research laboratories, companies that design medical devices, sports equipment, nanotechnology. They can also work in technical sales and technical writing creating user manuals, repair guides, test equipment
Electrical Engineering (EE)	Bachelor's Degree (engineer)	Investigate complex electrical problems and develop engineering methods to solve them.	Utility companies, government agencies, alternative energy companies, research laboratories, manufacturing plants, companies that design medical devices, sports equipment, nanotechnology

Degree comparison table of electrical engineering and electronic/electrical engineering technology.

ENVIRONMENTAL ENGINEERING

MEDIAN STARTING SALARY (FOR CIVIL ENGINEERING): $51,793
MEDIAN INCOME $80,890

Fresh air to breath, water to drink and healthy food to eat is usually the job of many types of engineers – primarily environmental, civil, chemical, manufacturing, and agricultural and biological engineers. It is easy to take air, water and food for granted if you have never been without them or never been exposed to people or places without them. However, having fresh air, water and healthy food is critical to continuing life on this planet.

Environmental engineering, which was often called sanitary engineering prior to 1970, focuses on the development of a sustainable future, preventing pollution, assessing the environmental impact of everything, water distribution systems, recycling methods, sewage treatment plants, and pesticide prevention. This fast-growing field offers a challenging and satisfying chance to protect the health and safety of people and our environment. These earth-friendly professionals concern themselves with preventing and fixing problems caused by industrialization. They concentrate on delivering better environmental conditions for the public through knowledge, research, a caring attitude, and common sense. One of the most rewarding aspects of being this type of engineer is that because there is such a large need for sustainability on every level, you can make a difference right away – from the first day on the job right through the rest of your career.

Air pollution is a problem worldwide. According to the World Health Organization, 70,000 people in the United States die from air pollution every year. That is twice as many as the number that die in traffic accidents.

Air quality has different effects on plants, animals and humans. In humans, poor air quality can lead to cancer, asthma and birth defects. Under the Clean Air Act, the Environmental Protection Agency (EPA) establishes primary air quality standards to protect public health, including the health of "sensitive" populations such as people with asthma, children, and older adults. The EPA also sets secondary standards to protect public welfare. This includes protecting ecosystems, including plants and animals, from harm, as well as protecting against decreased visibility and damage to crops, vegetation, and buildings.

Cleaning the air and water are usually jobs for environmental engineers. Environmental engineers use the principles of biology and chemistry to develop solutions to environmental problems. They are involved in water and air pollution control, recycling, waste disposal, and public health issues. Environmental engineers conduct hazardous-waste management studies in which they evaluate the significance of the hazard, advise on its treatment and containment, and develop regulations to prevent mishaps. They design municipal water supply and industrial wastewater treatment systems, conduct research on the environmental impact of proposed construction projects, analyze scientific data, and perform quality-control checks. Environmental engineers are concerned with local and worldwide environmental issues. Some may study and attempt to minimize the effects of acid rain, global warming, automobile emissions, and ozone depletion. They also may be involved in the protection of wildlife. Many environmental engineers work as consultants, helping their clients to comply with regulations, prevent environmental damage, and clean up hazardous sites.

These engineers must be excellent communicators and team players. They must able to work well with others because their work often includes collaborating with environmental scientists, urban planners, hazardous waste technicians, politicians, attorneys and other specialists. They prepare, review and update environmental investigations, provide clean-up recommendations, monitor projects, prepare forecasts and budgets and inspect sites for operational effectiveness and to ensure pollution compliance.

Environmental engineering education is a multi-disciplinary field. Students in this field will study mathematics, physics, biology, ecology, public health, geology, economics, politics, chemistry, and engineering design. Environmental engineering curriculum is very broad and requires that students understand how to apply engineering and scientific principles to the ailments of society.

FEATURE ARTICLE

THE FOOTSTEPS OF AN ENVIRONMENTAL ENGINEER - CHARLES WRIGHT, ENVIRONMENTAL ENGINEER FOR BROWN AND CALDWELL

After Charles Wright graduated from high school, he attended the University of Wyoming to study civil engineering. His father had an engineering degree, and it seemed like a logical choice for Charles since he was good at math and science. "Besides," he said, "I knew that I really wanted to work with water."

When Charles finished his bachelor's degree, he joined the Peace Corps and was sent to East Africa. "I had always been interested in the Peace Corps, and it gave me a chance to travel and do something worthwhile with my education." During the first year, Charles worked on a small pipeline project to supply water to a community in the area in which he lived. During his second year, Charles worked with small groups of women, training them to build concrete water tanks to catch and store rain water.

Charles's time in Africa with the Peace Corps increased his interest in water and in engineering. He decided to return to school to get a master's degree in environmental engineering at Clemson University.

Today, Charles works for a consulting environmental engineering firm. He focuses mainly on projects related to the expansion of municipal wastewater treatment facilities. Expansion of treatment plants is required to ensure adequate capacity for future growth of the communities and to ensure that the water quality standards as set by state and federal agencies are met. Typical projects involve millions of dollars and may take two years or more to complete.

Many large firms employ environmental engineers to decide how to dispose of toxic material or to control toxic emissions. Some environmental engineers inspect pollution control systems for the government; some design or inspect water treatment systems. Others develop and administer the regulations that protect health, safety, and the environment.

According to the American Academy of Environmental Engineers (AAEE), "Since environmental engineering is so intertwined with people, it is necessary that you understand how people and societies function. Through both your formal training and your activities during your college career, you need to work on developing your writing and speaking skills. Environmental engineers must be able to communicate effectively with people of all types if they are to succeed in solving problems. These skills can only be learned by doing – the more you do, the better you will become."

More information can be found at the AAEE website at www.aaee.net. For more information about environmental engineering and preparing to work as a civil/environmental engineer, pick up a copy of *From Sundaes to Space Stations: Careers in Civil Engineering* at engineeringedu.com.

FIRE PROTECTION ENGINEERING

STARTING SALARY: **$70,000**
MEDIAN INCOME: **$96,200**

"Fire protection engineering is the application of science, engineering principles and experience to protect people and their environments from the destructive effects of fire."
- The Society of Fire Protection Engineers (SFPE)

Fire protection engineers protect people, homes, the work place, industrial facilities and public spaces from the devastating effects of fire and explosion. They do this by evaluating fire safety and the design of fire safe systems in everything from vehicles to homes, buildings, and consumer products. This often involves computer modeling of the possible fire situations and innovative solutions that address the fire hazards, including the use of "smart" fire detectors and integrated smoke control systems, advanced fire suppression and special audible emergency communications for the occupants in the event of fire or explosion.

FPEs may work in the following scenarios:
1. They may work as spacecraft specialists making space travel safer for rocketeers and astronauts.
2. They may work as a fire safety specialist reviewing and testing products for fire fighter safety (clothing, breathing masks, etc).
3. They may work developing fire department programs.
4. They may work in disaster management ensuring the safety of people and the integrity of buildings in natural disasters such as earthquakes and floods.

5. They may be quality engineers inspecting all vehicles such as automobiles, large ocean going vessels, spacecraft, and aircraft for fire safety.
6. They may work as Fire Safety Development Engineers writing fire safety codes for buildings, homes and schools.
7. They may perform fire safety evaluations of buildings and industrial complexes to determine the risk of fire losses and how best to prevent them.
8. They may design systems that automatically detect and suppress fires and explosions as well as design fire alarm, smoke control, emergency lighting, communications and exit systems
9. They may conduct fire research on materials and consumer products and use computer modeling to predict fire growth and smoke behavior.
10. They may investigate fires or explosions, preparing technical reports or providing expert courtroom or government testimony.
11. They may survey major facilities and perform research, testing and analysis.

Most often, FPEs work in government agencies such as NASA, the CIA, the Navy, the Smithsonian Institute and the National Institute of Standards and Technology, healthcare facilities, large corporations, manufacturing facilities, insurance companies, civil engineering firms, and in consulting. They work "hand-in-hand" with architects, other engineers, government authorities, insurance underwriters, fire service personnel, lawyers and other FPE experts.

Fire Protection Engineering Technology

Median Starting Salary (for Fire Protection Engineering): $70,000

Median income (for Fire Protection Engineering): $96,200

In addition to Fire Protection Engineers there are also Fire Protection Engineering Technicians. These are highly specialized individuals, sometimes working as assistants to engineers, but more often working for fire protection contractors.

Fire Protection Engineering Technicians typically do detailed layout work for fire sprinkler systems, special fire suppression systems, and fire alarm systems. The work these technicians perform requires facility in CAD, knowledge of architectural drafting standards, the ability to read and interpret building and fire codes, and the ability to design something that installing technicians can actually build. A good STEM background is also necessary.

Another field where Fire Protection Engineering Technicians are often used is known as Inspection, Testing and Maintenance. Fire protection systems are of an emergency stand-by nature, and as with most stand-by equipment, they need regular attention and exercise to insure they will work when needed. Finding out the fire pump is not in proper working order when a fire breaks out is too late, so critical safety equipment is regularly inspected for good condition, tested to insure it will work properly when called on, and receive routine preventative maintenance.

Fire Protection Engineering Technicians may also work for large manufacturing corporations, and any of the other places where Fire Protection Engineers are employed.

Fire Protection Engineering Technicians attend both four-year and two-year colleges, depending on what they want to do, and usually work under supervision for a period of two to five years, and then must pass a battery of tests, before they are eligible for certification from the National Institute for the Certification of Engineering Technologies (NICET).

FOOD ENGINEERING

MEDIAN STARTING SALARY (FOR CHEMICAL ENGINEERING): $65,403
MEDIAN INCOME (FOR CHEMICAL ENGINEERING): $94,350

Take a walk down any aisle in your local grocery store. What most people don't realize is that behind every product on every shelf are engineers that work to make that food taste good and healthy. Every aspect of food production, processing, marketing, and distribution benefits from engineering.

Food engineers are involved in all aspects of food preparation and processing. They influence the packaging, storage, and distribution systems of foods as varied as candy bars and frozen dinners. Because new products and environmentally friendly food-processing equipment need to be developed, engineers are in demand within the food industry.

Food engineering pertains to the properties and characteristics of foods that affect their processing. Food engineering requires an understanding of the chemical, biochemical, microbiological, and physical characteristics of food. There will be a shortage of food engineers as long as society demands that engineers develop lower-fat, lower-salt, lower-cholesterol, or nutrient-packed foods for their diets.

FEATURE ARTICLE

FOOD FOR THOUGHT - THE ENGINEER WHO CAME TO DINNER

Remember when the frozen "TV dinner" was the only convenience food around? If you do, it's not so much a reflection of your age, as of the rapid changes in food technology. Whether they're more convenient, tastier, fresher, more nutritious, or just more fun, many of today's foods are engineering achievements.

What do engineers have to do with food? The question might actually be, what don't they? According to most reports, agriculture and food processing account for 20 percent of the nation's gross national product. Many of the 1.8 million engineers in the country work on getting food to your table every day, as well as on special things like Valentine's Day chocolates and food for astronauts on the Space Shuttle.

Of course, a food engineer's most important job is to ensure food safety, supply, nutrition, and stability. But, beyond these basics, engineers continue to work to make food tastier, more convenient, and more appealing.

While TV dinners, now 42 years old, may not inspire the excitement they once did, even some recent innovations are pretty much taken for granted. One example is TetraPak juice boxes, which combine added convenience with improved product quality and stability.

Recently, with concerns about landfill capacity, engineers have looked more closely at how to make food packaging more environmentally friendly.

Everyone's familiar with decaffeinated coffee. Yet how many realize that engineers developed the super critical carbon dioxide process to remove caffeine from coffee without using traditional hydrocarbon solvents? Now, we can all sleep better.

And, what about the ubiquitous microwave and microwavable food, not to mention freeze-dried and dehydrated foods, boil in a bag, and all the other forms of food packaging? All were developed by engineers.

To wash all this food down, you might drink milk bought right off the grocery shelf, without refrigeration. Using ultra-high temperature processing, engineers have developed a way to keep milk fresh longer, even at room temperature. Of course, this is just the latest development in a series of engineered advances for milk that includes vitamin fortification and lactose-free and low-fat varieties.

For dessert, how about some engineered ice cream? Frozen desserts, like ice cream, have presented unique challenges to engineers. Ice cream is a three-phase emulsion system (oil, water, and air) which has to be delicately balanced to provide the desired product characteristics.

Processing conditions such as freezing rate influence the rate of ice crystal formation and have an effect on the resulting texture and "mouthfeel" of the product. Formulation plays a role as well, when different flavors, fruits, and colors are added, the balance of the system is altered.

Food provides a special challenge to engineers, because it is not as simple as other systems where physical and chemical properties are well defined and compositions known. Most foods are complex mixtures made up of thousands of compounds. Although food's chemical components can be broadly categorized as proteins, carbohydrates, fats, vitamins, minerals, flavors, and enzymes, this simplification does not truly reflect the variety of compounds within each class.

What complicates matters more is that the compounds all interact with each other. And, processing food in the plant or cooking it at home changes the flavor, color, and nutritional characteristics.

Food engineers are also involved in cutting-edge technologies, like genetic engineering, to produce crops more resistant to pests, or more durable for processing. In processing, newer technologies such as freeze drying or supercritical extraction are used in cases where maintaining heat-liable compounds (such as flavors) are important.

How is a typical new food "engineered?" After a product concept is developed in a lab, it is done "bench-scale," where there is close control of composition and processing. One of the engineer's tasks is to translate a lab process to large-scale production. The product also has to be packaged in a way to ensure easy distribution and preparation. And, through the entire interval, from the time the product leaves the plant until it is served at the table, it must maintain its quality.

Established products must be continually "re-engineered" to give them advantages over the competition. These include better overall flavor (or more variety), making the packaging more recyclable, reducing manufacturing costs, improving nutrition, or innovations for added convenience.

Reprinted courtesy of The American Institute of Chemical Engineers.

HEATING, VENTILATING, REFRIGERATING, AND AIR-CONDITIONING ENGINEERING

MEDIAN STARTING SALARY (FOR MECHANICAL ENGINEERING): $58,600
MEDIAN INCOME (FOR MECHANICAL ENGINEERING): $80,580

Heating, ventilating, refrigeration, and air-conditioning (HVR&AC) engineers have dramatically improved our lives. HVR&AC engineers develop systems to create and maintain safe and comfortable environments. Airplanes, trains, schools, cars, and computer rooms are only a handful of the environments that depend on HVR&AC engineers.

An HVR&AC engineer who has an interest in biology can develop cryosurgery systems. An HVR&AC engineer with an interest in transportation can develop refrigerator cars for trains and trucks to enable transportation of chemicals or freezer foods.

An HVR&AC engineer with an interest in energy conservation can design more efficient heating, ventilating, refrigeration, or air-conditioning systems. Visit the American Society of Heating, Refrigerating and Air-Conditioning Engineers website at www. ashrae.org for more information.

FEATURE ARTICLE

REFRIGERATION, MILTON GARLAND: ONE "COOL" ENGINEER (A TRIBUTE)

What do ice cubes, air conditioning, computers, hockey, antibiotics, organ transplants, space exploration, and fresh fruit have in common? To answer that question, look around you. Almost everywhere you look you will see the positive impact of refrigeration technology. One of the giants of the heating, ventilating, air-conditioning and refrigerating industry is refrigeration engineer and inventor Milton W. Garland. For over 77 years, he advanced refrigeration technology through his inventions and his public service. In fact, Garland, who lived over 100 years, is known throughout the industry as "Mr. Refrigeration."

Garland held 40 patents and was the developer of refrigeration compressors for industrial and commercial use. But, Garland's most recognizable invention was the first "shell" ice maker, which manufactured ice on the outside of four-inch diameter, ten-foot length tubes. His system was more efficient and sanitary than the then-current system of producing ice in galvanized cans. As a result, demand soared for use in chicken processing plants, for cooling milk containers during deliveries, and developing an industrial air conditioning system in a two-mile deep gold mine, which reduced temperatures from 110 degrees to 90 degrees F.

Garland obtained his first experience with refrigeration engineering in the U.S. Navy during World War I. In 1920, he graduated from Worcester

Polytechnic Institute in Massachusetts, and joined the Frick Company, in Waynesboro, Pennsylvania. Over the next half century, he served in the positions of field installation trainee, chief engineer, vice president of engineering, and vice president of technical services.

Of his career Garland says, "I wanted to be an engineer ever since I was a little boy. Someway, somehow, I was going to be an engineer."

Garland played golf once a week, and was an avid hockey fan. And why not? He helped engineer the refrigeration system for the Hershey Bears' ice rink in Hershey, Pennsylvania. He and his wife, Alice, were known to drive 140 miles round trip during the winter to see a home game.

Reprinted courtesy of the American Society of Heating, Refrigerating and Air-Conditioning Engineers, Inc.

Industrial Engineering

Median Starting salary: $58,581
Median Income: $78,860

Industrial engineers figure out how to improve everything. They work with people and companies to help them be more efficient. Industrial engineers save employers money by streamlining systems, often making the workplace better for employees too. They improve productivity and quality while saving time and money.

Industrial engineers work on all type of businesses. They see the big picture and focus on what makes a system perform efficiently, safely, and effectively to produce the highest quality. They often work with or are closely associated with manufacturing engineers.

According to the Institute of Industrial Engineers (IIE), "Industrial engineering (IE) is about choices. Other engineering disciplines apply skills to very specific areas. IE gives you the opportunity to work in a variety of businesses. The most distinctive aspect of industrial engineering is the flexibility that it offers. Whether it's shortening a roller coaster line, streamlining an operating room, distributing products worldwide, or manufacturing superior automobiles, all share the common goal of saving companies money and increasing efficiencies."

Industrial engineers work in many different types of organizations. They apply their special skills in hospitals, banks, manufacturing plants, insurance companies, or government agencies. Major employers of industrial engineers include corporations such as Microsoft, Boeing, Disney, Intel, and Nike. And the list goes on.

As an industrial engineer, you may look for new ways to do things better. You may try to automate agencies so that their customers don't have to wait in long lines. You may find ways to make sure employees always have what they need to complete their job. You may survey locations to find the best place to build a major facility.

The Institute of Industrial Engineers (IIE) has a website at www.iienet.org that is full of great information for students. The Institute recognizes outstanding students, offers several scholarships, and has annual competitions.

INDUSTRIAL ENGINEERING TECHNOLOGY
AVERAGE STARTING SALARY (BACHELOR'S DEGREE): $42,634
MEDIAN INCOME: $50,980

Industrial engineering technologists and technicians plan ways to effectively use personnel, materials, and machines in factories, stores, hospitals, repair shops, and offices. As assistants to industrial engineers, they help prepare machinery and equipment layouts, plan workflows, conduct statistical production studies, and analyze production costs. They may act as the eyes and ears of the industrial engineer as they

conduct time studies, work place design, and accommodations under OSHA and the Americans with Disabilities Act.

If you want to work in company productivity, industrial engineering is a great choice. Industrial engineering technology is very similar to manufacturing engineering technology. The difference is that industrial engineering technologists focus on knowing how to work with people and systems to make products faster, cheaper and better whereas manufacturing engineering technologists focus on how to use machines to make those same products. Manufacturing engineering technologists focus on knowing machine tooling, Computer-Aided-Design, CNC Programming, etc. and industrial engineering technologists focus on the people using the machines. They assess the psychology of the workplace, ergonomic issues, and other problems that have the potential to limit production quality and efficiency. Industrial engineering technology is a degree that is especially appropriate for people who want to work with other people.

Industrial engineering technologists and technicians work with engineers to customize existing manufacturing processes related to the manufacturing of products. They plan, test, produce, and fabricate consumer and industrial products and can serve as a communications bridge between the shop floor and management. They may find themselves working in various industries and businesses to coordinate activities that ensure the quality of final products or services. They strive to improve manufacturing processes, product quality and per piece profits – all with an eye towards employee efficiency, productivity and safety.

They may find themselves planning, designing, testing, and analyzing processes and systems, inspecting operations, running tests on particular areas of the system, managing projects, supervising production lines, writing reports, communicating with other members on the team, and giving presentations about their findings.

Industrial engineering technologists are trouble-shooters who take the engineers' design or concept and turn it into a product with attention to manufacturability, quality assurance, and cost-effective production using engineering principles, computers and software along with their practical technical skills. It is an exciting field rich in opportunities not only locally or statewide, but all over the world.

Students can also attend two-year colleges and graduate with an associate's degree to become a technician or continue to the bachelor's degree. Although the schooling to become an engineering technologist is still four years, it is slightly less calculus intensive than industrial engineering. The focus is on hands-on experience and the application of ideas using scientific principles. The two extra years of education that separates a technologist from a technician provides significant opportunities for advancement into management of manufacturing engineering systems, production operations, or technical sales.

MANUFACTURING ENGINEERING
MEDIAN STARTING SALARY: $58,581
MEDIAN INCOME (FOR MECHANICAL ENGINEERING): $80,580

Just as the mechanical engineer designs parts, the manufacturing engineer designs the processes that make them. You find manufacturing engineers in Detroit's big-three production facilities, overseeing plants of the major computer companies, directing six-person mold and die shops that make advanced prototypes, and working on teams in the football-field-sized structures where Boeing assembles jumbo jets. Wherever there's a production process to be designed and managed, you'll find manufacturing engineers at work.

Manufacturing engineers need an aptitude for basic engineering principles, a disciplined approach to work, and creativity. Because the focus is the process, not the individual part, they need to look through a wider-angle lens. They bring their particular brand of insight to teams. They work with plant managers, production supervisors, CNC programmers, quality managers, product designers, and R&D staff on issues ranging from evaluating new technology and choosing equipment and suppliers to leading industry-wide standards development to reorganizing a plant into a more efficient production system.

Negotiation skills and the ability to sell ideas are essential. Ford Motor Co. names interpersonal skills right after basic engineering on the list of skills manufacturing engineers need. Ford's manufacturing engineers must work closely with product designers and communicate with them on the same technical level. The goal is not to make a designer out of the manufacturing engineer, but to get design and manufacturing to work seamlessly together to make products of the highest quality at the lowest possible cost.

During the last two decades, most major U.S. companies have turned their attention to the plant floor, discovering that the way they make their products can be a strategic advantage in the growing global marketplace. Manufacturing engineers led the way by championing key concepts including lean production, agile manufacturing, re-engineering, and continuous improvement.

Manufacturing engineers must do more than make and deliver products competitively. They must use system thinking to understand what role manufacturing plays in the overall business and how to customize products to meet the needs and suit the tastes of customers around the world.

The Society of Manufacturing Engineers (SME) certifies manufacturing engineers (CmfgE) and technologists (CMfgT). In most states, a state-sponsored examination leads to professional registration in manufacturing engineering.

To attract young people to the field, SME sponsors an annual student robotics/automation contest with hundreds of entries from middle school through college (www.sme.org).

MANUFACTURING ENGINEERING TECHNOLOGY
THE AVERAGE STARTING SALARY FOR A GRADUATE WITH:
MANUFACTURING ENGINEERING TECHNOLOGY (BACHELOR'S DEGREE) $42,634
MANUFACTURING ENGINEERING TECHNOLOGY (ASSOCIATE'S DEGREE) $29,175

Manufacturing engineering technologists and technicians work with engineers to customize existing manufacturing processes related to the manufacturing of products. They plan, test, produce, and fabricate consumer and industrial products and can serve as a communications bridge between the shop floor and management. They may find themselves developing processes for a small office to manufacturing systems in football field sized buildings. Regardless of the size of the business Manufacturing engineering technologists and technicians are tasked with continually improving the manufacturing process to improve product quality and improve per piece profits.

Manufacturing Engineering Technology is an exciting career path focused on the application of technology in high-tech environments, using computer-aided design, CNC operations, robotics, lasers, and microprocessor controls to manufacture the products that society needs and wants. Technologists and technicians

may find themselves planning, designing, testing, and analyzing processes and systems, inspecting operations, running tests on particular areas of the system, managing projects, supervising production lines, writing reports, communicating with other members on the team, and giving presentations about their findings.

Technologists are involved in all stages of design and manufacturing and work in a wide variety of firms – a few of these include aerospace and telecommunications companies, sports equipment companies and consumer product related companies. These graduates may work in manufacturing facilities; federal, state or local government agencies, such as the U.S. Postal Service; medical device companies; computer equipment companies; and many more. Technologists are well-prepared to perform in such positions as manufacturing engineer, quality assurance engineer, production engineer, project engineer, and facilities engineer. They may also work in technical sales and technical services, representing manufacturers of production equipment.

Although the schooling to become an engineering technologist is still four years, it is slightly less calculus intensive than manufacturing engineering. The focus is on hands-on experience and the application of ideas using scientific principles. Graduates will have an excellent understanding of casting, forming, machining, and fabricating processes that are used by today's leading manufacturing companies. The two extra years of education that separates a technologist from a technician provides

significant opportunities for advancement into management of manufacturing engineering, production operations, or technical sales. According to the National Center for Manufacturing Education (NCME), "The career advancement potential for BSET graduates within manufacturing enterprises generally is limited only by the individual's personal abilities to lead, diligence in keeping up-to-date in technical knowledge, and the knowledge of modern manufacturing techniques."

- A technologist with an interest in business may estimate labor costs, equipment life and facility space requirements.
- Depending on the employer, a technologist with an interest in design may work on the processes that create consumer products, such as candy, motorcycles, kitchen equipment, snowboards, music technologies, military ships and aircraft, and wireless devices.
- Technologists may also work in food technology to make sure your breakfast cereal or frozen waffles are delivered to the right supermarket on time, on budget, and are processed efficiently.

Students can also attend two-year colleges and graduate with an associate's degree to become a technician or continue to the bachelor's degree. Technicians work for the same companies and are the hands-on people involved in the installation, maintenance and repair of the same manufacturing and control systems and processes. They are trouble-shooters who take the engineers' design or concept and turn it into a product with attention to manufacturability, quality assurance, and cost-effective production using engineering principles, computers and software along with their practical technical skills. It is an exciting field rich in opportunities not only locally or statewide, but all over the world. According to *A Novel Curriculum for the Associate Degree in Manufacturing Engineering Technology,* by the National Center of Excellence for Advanced Manufacturing Education, "Compared with the high school graduate, the associate degree graduate would possess higher levels of knowledge and skill in mathematics, science, humanities, communications, computer use, and the technologies of manufacturing. On-the-job experience should prepare the graduate to take more responsibility for the planning and implementation of continuous improvements to operations. The manufacturing engineering technician would work as a key person supporting the team of people responsible for the manufacture of products and systems within the overall structure of a manufacturing enterprise. Primary tasks would involve assisting and supporting production planning and control, production operations management, quality management, manufacturing systems planning and management, and maintenance management."

There are three choices for majoring in manufacturing engineering technology or manufacturing engineering. The table on the following page gives a basic understanding of the differences but both sections on manufacturing engineering and manufacturing engineering technology should be read to gain a more thorough understanding of the fields and the differences between them.

Degree Program	Degree Type	Primary Focus	Types of employers
Manufacturing Engineering Technology	Associate's Degree (technician)	Installation, maintenance and repair of manufacturing and control systems and processes. Takes design or concept and turn it into a product with attention to manufacturability, quality assurance, and cost-effective production. Cannot be licensed as a PE.	Manufacturing facilities; federal, state or local government agencies, such as the U.S. Postal Service; medical device companies; computer equipment companies; and many more.
Manufacturing Engineering Technology	Bachelor's Degree (engineering technologist)	Applies technology in high-tech environments, using computer-aided design, CNC operations, robotics, lasers, and microprocessor controls to manufacture the products that society needs and wants, Designs and develops manufacturing machines and processes	Manufacturing facilities; government agencies, research labs, medical device companies, computer equipment companies
Manufacturing Engineering	Bachelor's Degree (engineer)	Investigate complex manufacturing problems and develop engineering methods to solve them.	Manufacturing facilities; government agencies, research labs; medical device and computer equipment companies

Degree comparison table of manufacturing engineering and manufacturing engineering technology.

MARINE ENGINEERING

STARTING SALARY (FOR MECHANICAL ENGINEERING): $ 58,749
MEDIAN INCOME: $88,100

Naval architects may design the frame or structure of a boat, but marine engineers design all of the internal power and machinery systems in the boat. Without marine engineers, the boat would have no engine, electronics, hydraulics, lighting, refrigeration, or controls. According to Jose Femenia, a professor of Marine Engineering at the United States Merchant Marine Academy,

> *"Marine Engineering is a very strong energy conversion discipline and very broad based. The subjects learned can be applied to shore side industries as well as the marine industry. I strongly recommend it, especially if you are interested in boats and/or ships." Because most boats cannot be designed without regard to the control systems, marine engineers often work closely with naval architects."*

To be a good marine engineer, you must be versatile, creative, and open to learning. Marine engineering is an exciting career because every boat or ship is different, and you will be responsible for every system on board. Almost every boat needs an engine, propeller, steering, transmission, pumps, electrical systems, etc. Marine engineers make it all happen. They understand the needs of the unique environment and know many different kinds of boating systems and controls.

Marine engineers determine and design different types of engines to propel a boat such as electric engines, diesel engines, steam turbines, water jets, gas turbines, and nuclear reactors. They also design hydraulic systems that can lift a 300 lb Marlin or crab nets out of the water for fishing boats, and the automated refrigeration systems for cruise lines  or other pleasure yachts. Marine engineers may find themselves designing the electrical or fluid systems on an aircraft carrier, or the mechanical control systems on a tugboat or other bay-, lake-, swamp- or ocean-going vessel. There are almost no systems on a maritime vessel that they don't have a hand in designing.

Marine engineers and naval architects may work on a ship at sea, in a shipyard, in factories where marine machinery is built, in design offices, in ship owners' offices, or for government agencies including military services.

Alan Rowen, technical director for The Society of Naval Architects and Marine Engineers (SNAME) and professor emeritus of marine engineering at the Webb Institute of Naval Architecture, explains that the sea-going engineers aboard ships tend to the operation and maintenance of the ship's machinery. They will also be responsible for the unlicensed crew working under their supervision. They may be in charge of an emergency team, damage-control team, or a life-boat. As the ship is traveling across the ocean, the sea-going, watch-standing engineer tends the machinery in the engine room of a ship for two, four-hour watches each day with eight hours off in between. They may use hand tools and machine tools, cutting and welding equipment, and machinery of all  types—all while not getting seasick! In addition, computer skills are absolutely necessary. They must possess:

- Good mechanical aptitude,
- An ability to visualize systems in three dimensions,
- An ability to think things through in a logical manner,
- Good common sense,
- Persistence,
- Willingness to learn,
- An open mind, and
- An ability to clearly express ideas verbally, graphically, and in writing.

Sea-going marine engineers and naval architects, as well as those stationed overseas managing new construction or major repairs, may miss their family life at home, and a ship at sea can be dangerous and uncomfortable in heavy weather. On the other hand, sea-going engineers typically have more days off. Usually, for every seven days at sea, they may get four days at home. Whether they are in a shipyard or at sea, marine engineers and naval architects must be physically fit to meet the demands of the job.

LICENSES

There are a few types of licenses necessary to be a marine engineer.

1. Sea-going engineers start with a third assistant engineer's license, issued by the U.S. Coast Guard to those who meet the requirements of classroom instruction and practical experience aboard a ship. The exam may take several days to complete.

2. Many naval architects and marine engineers are licensed Professional Engineers, and some are certified marine surveyors.

3. Many marine engineers are sea-going marine engineers licensed by the U.S. Coast Guard or other national regulatory bodies.

When you think of marine engineers, think of them as the keymakers of the ship world. Without a key, you can't even get onboard and you certainly can't go anywhere. They give millions of people the ability to have fun on a Jet Ski, small sailboat, or vacation cruise, as well as enabling the military to race across the oceans, clean-up oil spills, and rescue boats in distress.

For more information about marine engineering and preparing to work as a marine engineer, visit the Society of Naval Architects and Marine Engineers at www.sname.org or pick up a copy of *The Maritime Engineer: Careers in Naval Architecture and Marine, Ocean and Naval Engineering* at engineeringedu.com.

MARINE ENGINEERING TECHNOLOGY

Marine Engineering Technology is a multidisciplinary degree that combines marine engineering, engine repair and maintenance, power systems, and the mechanical and electrical systems of ships. Graduates of such programs usually work aboard commercial and military vessels, posts and drilling rigs on:

- Power cycles
- Principles and methods used to convert available energy into useful power
- Selection and operation of major components of power-related machinery
- Support systems for the power cycle

Marine engineering technologists and technicians also know the basics of naval architecture, marine applications of electrical engineering, and instrumentation. They may be involved with offshore drilling platforms, harbor facilities, breakwaters, and shipboard or underwater machines and devices. Because students are often trained on marine vessels during school, most programs are located near coastal or inland waterways.

Marine Engineering Technology is taught as an associate's degree but is usually a bachelor's degree program, which typically includes earning a U.S. Coast Guard License as a Third Assistant engineer on a commercial vessel. Students are often trained aboard a ship during school and the degree also qualifies an individual to earn a terminal license as a Chief Engineer in the commercial shipping industry. There are six state Maritime Academies and one national Maritime Academy at King's Point, NY.

There are three choices for majoring in marine engineering technology or marine engineering. The table below gives a basic understanding of the differences but both sections on marine engineering and marine engineering technology should be read to gain a more thorough understanding of the fields and the differences between them.

Degree Program	Degree Type	Primary Focus	Types of employers
Marine Engineering Technology	Associate's Degree (technician)	Repair and maintain mechanical and electrical systems and equipment on any type of vessel, oil rig, platform or dock.	All companies that design, develop, and/ or manufacture boating equipment, instrumentation, boat engines, and scuba equipment. The US Navy and forms that contract for the Navy are also large employers.
Marine Engineering Technology	Bachelor's Degree (engineering technologist)	Manage and support the design, manufacture and use of shipboard equipment, devices and technology.	Boat, ship, and yacht design and manufacturing companies; instrumentation, boat engines, and scuba equipment companies; Research labs; oil rig companies; the US Navy and companies that contract for the Navy are also large employers.
Marine Engineering	Bachelor's Degree (engineer)	Investigate complex shipboard systems problems and develop engineering methods to solve them. Manage and support the design, manufacture and use of shipboard equipment, devices and technology.	Boat, ship, and yacht design and manufacturing companies; instrumentation, boat engines, and scuba equipment companies; Research labs; oil rig companies; the US Navy and companies that contract for the Navy are also large employers.

Degree comparison table of marine engineering and marine engineering technology.

MATERIALS ENGINEERING

STARTING SALARY: $62,000
MEDIAN INCOME: $85,150

Materials engineers design, fabricate, and test materials. They may work to make automobiles lighter and more fuel efficient by creating stronger and lighter metals. They may help to create artificial knees and elbows using special polymers, or they may design new materials for the next space shuttle.

A materials engineer can work with any type of material – plastic, wood, ceramic, petroleum, or metals – and create completely new synthetic products by rearranging the molecular structure. For example, Teflon (polytetrafluoroethylene), the product that coats millions of cooking pans, was invented by freezing and compressing a gas related to refrigerants.

Materials engineers have numerous career opportunities available to them. Materials can lead to a career in the transportation industry, for example, working to design more fuel-efficient cars, trains, boats, and buses. Special lubrication products can be designed for race car suspensions and high-strength alloys for space travel. Materials engineering can also lead  to a career in communications. Semiconductor companies employ materials engineers to develop silicone to speed up computers by allowing faster transport of electronic signals. New and purer forms of germanium, cesium, tungsten, and copper used in electronic components also need to be developed to lower the cost and increase the stability of all electronic components and systems.

As stated on the San Jose State University materials engineering department website, "The percentage of materials engineers in the total of all engineers in the engineering profession is small: probably less than 5 percent. However, the need to apply basic materials principles to the solution of engineering problems is great. Certainly in today's high-tech society basic materials principles must be applied to almost all endeavors: thermal protection of the space shuttle; creation of the artificial hip; design of the titanium golf club; and production of advanced battery systems for the electric car, the artificial heart, and the laptop computer. Industry and government have traditionally depended on a few individuals on a project to address, for example, materials selection and process issues (i.e., a titanium, stainless steel or plastic artificial hip; which alloy; which fabrication sequence; a protective coating for corrosion and wear). Without the benefit of a materials education, these individuals rely on handbook information, experience and vendor data to select materials and to determine the processing sequence. The B.S. degree in materials science and engineering teaches the inter-relationship between structure, properties and processing; factors which determine the in-service performance and durability of a component or product."

FEATURE ARTICLE

SMART ENGINEERING
Smart engineering doesn't have so much to do with being a smart engineer as it does to creating smart structures or materials with a brain. "What does that mean?" you may ask. Think about the last time you saw the downhill ski competition in the Olympics. Do you remember how fast those skiers were flying? Do you remember watching their skis scream right through all that powder or watching in horror as the ice-packed snow sent a contestant toppling down the hill at 70 m.p.h.?

What if you could make a difference in the performance of the Olympic participants? What if you could improve skiers' performance, making them faster by allowing more control? What if you could create a product that allowed professionals to break the current world records?

To give you some background, let's talk about what it takes to design skis. Ski designs vary to accommodate different environmental conditions. Longer skis provide more stability and allow for more control at higher speeds, while shorter skis are better for turning in any condition because there is less ski to manage. However, short skis also have a tendency to vibrate and cause a loss of control. Wider skis distribute your weight over a larger area and are therefore better for soft powdery snow. To ski on hard-packed snow, a rider wants an hourglass ski that digs deeper and makes sharper cuts.

If the sporting goods industry is your destiny, smart materials technology may be your ticket. Smart skis use piezoelectric devices (special sensors) to detect vibration and act like a shock absorber, thereby getting rid of vibration. With less vibration, skiers can control their rides better and are thus able to go faster and make quicker turns. The sensors acts like the human body's nerve endings, except the sensors absorb vibration and convert the shock or vibration into electrical charge. A tiny control circuit then releases the energy through heat and light, eliminating vibrations. With reduced vibrations, more of the ski stays in contact with the snow; the result is greater stability, higher speed, and smoother riding.

For example, when you ride in a car you have optimum control over the vehicle when all four tires are on the road. If you make a turn very fast and two tires come off the road, you have lost control and are probably holding on for dear life. A professional race car has very wide tires to enable more traction and keep the driver in full control at the fastest possible speed. The same theory holds true for amateur and professional skiers: you have the most control when the entire surface area of the ski is touching the snow.

How does it work?
Piezoelectric devices, the sensors that make a snowboard smart, have the unique ability to detect a shock or vibration and convert it into an electric charge. The piezos are manufactured right into the snowboard. On hard-packed snow, snowboards are especially prone to vibration. These vibrations lessen stability, control, and overall performance.

The piezo control module takes the mechanical energy produced from the vibration and converts it into electrical energy. The electrical energy is applied across a shunt circuit that transforms it into heat and removes it from the board to reduce the vibration. Look at it this way: If you have $300 and then buy a snowboard, you now have a snowboard instead of $300. If you have vibration and trade it for heat, you now have heat instead of vibration. The vibration is gone and the heat is simply transferred out. The applications of smart engineering are limitless and will change the way we live.

Currently, smart materials are also used in other sports equipment such as baseball bats, water skis, and mountain bikes. Any sport you can think of where less vibration would increase performance is a market for smart materials. It is being used in building design to accommodate mother nature's fury. Even smart clothes have hit the scene.

Smart Structures
The multidisciplinary field of smart engineering comprises scientific knowledge about materials, sensors, constructions, electronics, mechanics, and information processing. Smart materials are defined as materials that react and modify their reaction because of changes in the environment – like the smart skis, snowboards, and mountain bikes discussed earlier. Smart structures are understood as the system of sensors and actuators that keep the structure in a current state (standing upright) or aid the structure's reaction to a particular event (hurricane winds).

If we want to have a smart structure, we have to make it smart. For example, suppose you are the lead civil engineer on a bridge project. As the engineer responsible for the safe transportation of millions of people every week, you want to know when the bridge shows any signs of decay, deterioration, or damage.

Smart technology can do just that. Sensors can be embedded in the concrete structure to sense changes in pressure and signal when structural damage may occur. Any structure that undergoes a lot of wear and tear is a potential applicant for smart technology. Engineers hope to save both time and lives with smart structures that warn the operator or designer when weak spots present a potential disaster.

Eventually, earthquake resistant structures will also be possible. A smart structure will sense an earthquake and the building materials will actually alter their stiffness in response to the movement of the earth. Smart structures will shake the building in the opposite direction of the earth's movement and thereby cancel out the effects of the quake.

Other Smart Stuff

Other applications for smart materials include space structures, airplanes, helicopters, submarines, the sound industry, the automobile industry, and artificial muscles, and more. Anything that can be improved by increased performance, greater stability, or decreased maintenance is a candidate for smart technology.

Space Structures – Large space structures are subject to a variety of disturbances by the crew, the docking of other spacecraft, temperature changes during the orbit, and tiny meteorites. Smart materials can damp the vibrations of the disturbances to avoid instability and achieve optimum control in the space structure.

Airplanes – Airplanes that have smart materials embedded in their bodies will have control surfaces that can reshape themselves in mid flight. With the help of the smart structures airfoil, the shape and lift of the aircraft will be improved. A single-engine fighter could fly off the deck of an aircraft carrier without a catapult when this technology becomes available. Lightweight and high performance smart materials could double an aircraft's flight range and require 30 percent less fuel.

Helicopter Blades – Helicopter blades can adjust their shape continuously to respond to air-pressure changes that cause vibrations. Those fluctuations knock the machinery out of alignment and cause a helicopter to require excessive maintenance. Piezoelectric patches on the blade surfaces can function as both sensors and actuators, or generators of counter-force.

Submarines – Smart materials technology may result in stealth submarines. Their smart skins would detect the pressure of an incoming sonar wave and automatically generate an equal but opposite counter pressure that would cancel out the ping. With nothing reflected back to the enemy boat, the submarine would be invisible.

Auto Industry – The automotive industry incorporates intelligent materials technology in projects such as smart car seats that can identify primary occupants and adapt to their preferences for height, legroom, back support, and so forth. Smart materials will also lead to new kinds of suspensions and transmissions.

Sound Industry – Speaker research is aimed at turning whole house walls or car interiors into speakers by embedding them with tiny actuators. Fifty years from now people won't need to install separate speakers in their homes and cars in an attempt to achieve dramatic sound effects. Their cars and houses will offer built-in surround-sound.

Artificial Muscles – Smart materials that expand and contract similar to human muscles have already been embedded in prosthetic arms and could find numerous applications in robotics, medical implants, and virtual reality.

The field of smart materials is growing rapidly and may be an exciting way to stay on the cutting-edge of technology for many years to come.

More information about materials engineering can be found at the Society for Biomaterials website at www.biomaterials.org, the Materials Engineering and Sciences Division of the AIChE site at www.aiche.org, the Materials Engineering Division of the ASCE site at www.asce.org, and the Materials Division of the ASME site at www.asme.org.

MECHANICAL ENGINEERING

MEDIAN STARTING SALARY: $58,600
MEDIAN INCOME: $80,580

Mechanical engineers are the wheels of the world. The majority of people in this career are concerned with the motion of everything: from automobile wheels and systems, to roller coasters, to the inner workings of machines, to the motions of microscopic particles in a nanotechnology research facility or laboratory. This type of engineering is one of the broadest, oldest, and most diverse disciplines. Almost every object you used today was the handiwork of a mechanical engineer. Their creations can directly or indirectly benefit society and make an impact on all of us. Not many people can perform their jobs without them. Mechanical engineers use the principles of energy, mechanics, materials, mathematics, and engineering sciences to research, design, develop, test, and manufacture every kind of vehicle, power system, machine, and technological system: jet engines, steam engines, power plants, underwater structures, tractors for food production, hydraulic systems, transportation systems, medical devices, energy systems, sports equipment, smart materials, materials and structures for space travel, manufacturing processes, measurement devices, and more. Any type of machine that produces, transmits, or uses power is most likely the product of a mechanical engineer. They can work in testing, quality assurance, manufacturing, research, design, development, operations, management, production, marketing, sales, or product maintenance for large companies, small firms, or for themselves as consultants. There is hardly any aspect of life that has not been influenced by a mechanical engineer.

According to the Department of Labor, by the year 2018, there will be an extra 87,000 jobs for mechanical engineers and mechanical engineering is also listed as one of the top 50 occupations with the most openings that requires a bachelor's degree. The job is highly individualistic and flexible because it is so broad. Because so many companies and government facilities need machines and systems to be more competitive in today's global marketplace, graduates will find a substantially increased ability to make great money doing what they want and living where they want.

These trends include:

- The creation of new materials featuring remarkable attributes of strength and lightness.
- The miniaturization of medical instruments and other tools.
- Flexible and programmable manufacturing systems allowing rapid switching from one product to another.
- Energy technologies development such as fuel cells, solar energy, wind farm development, more fuel efficient or alternative energy transportation systems, and management of environmental waste and hazards in compliance with stringent government regulations.
- Enhancement of the role of personal computers in engineering design and analysis.

As well, an increasing number of mechanical engineers will be needed to design and develop devices for the general public that will make their lives more convenient, cost effective, easier, more efficient, and more comfortable. These products can be anything from washers and dryers to cell phones and other electronic gadgets, to airplanes and other transportation.

Since mechanical engineering is such a broad discipline, select a school whose area of emphasis matches your own interests. For example, if you are interested in automotive engineering and wish to broaden your choice of schools, select a college that teaches mechanical engineering with an emphasis in automotive engineering such as the University of Illinois, Michigan, or Tennessee. If your primary interest is to make cars or any vehicle go faster, choose a school with an emphasis in combustion, materials, fluid mechanics, or thermodynamics. If you are interested in mechanical engineering and also biomedical engineering and want to work on hospital equipment, you can specialize in electrical engineering. Or choose an emphasis in chemical engineering if you want to work in the pharmaceutical industry. Mechanical engineers can also work on joint replacements such as artificial knees, hips, or elbows.

A great way to become more familiar with mechanical engineering is to check out the various divisions within the ASME website (www.asme.org). This list is an important learning tool because you will be able to clearly see the enormous impact that mechanical engineering has on our world. Essentially, you can combine almost any other technical interest such as internal combustion, computers, telecommunications, biomedical engineering, mechanics, materials, nuclear energy, alternative energy, noise control, aerospace, and much more with a degree in mechanical engineering.

MECHANICAL ENGINEERING TECHNOLOGY

THE AVERAGE STARTING SALARY FOR A GRADUATE WITH:
BACHELOR'S DEGREE IN MECHANICAL ENGINEERING TECHNOLOGY IS $37,500
ASSOCIATE'S DEGREE IN MECHANICAL ENGINEERING TECHNOLOGY IS $31,250

Mechanical engineering technologists and technicians work with engineers to design, develop, manufacture, and test various kinds of machines, components, and products. Anything with moving parts falls under the domain of mechanical engineering and mechanical engineering technology. Technologists and technicians may find themselves planning, designing, testing operating and analyzing machines, processes and installations. They may inspect operations, maintain, install or operate components, or run tests on parts and equipment in a laboratory. They may also write reports, communicate with other members on the team and give presentations about their findings.

Mechanical engineering technologists are heavily involved with different aspects of design – solid modeling, finite-element analysis, tolerance stack-up, mechanism synthesis, etc. They are involved in manufacturing and may work in consulting firms; manufacturing facilities; federal, state, or local government agencies (such as Federal Aviation Administration and the Department of Defense); material  testing laboratories; medical device companies; computer equipment companies or service providers; telecommunications companies; utility companies; and many more.

Mechanical engineering technicians may work for the same companies as mechanical engineers and engineering technologists, and may be involved in the installation, maintenance, and repair of machines, manufacturing systems, and control systems. They are the hands-on people - trouble-shooters - that use available materials, engineering principles, and their practical technical skills to take the engineers' design or concept and turn it into a machine, system or product. It is an exciting field that is rich in opportunities, not only locally or statewide but also all over the world.

- A technologist who works in quality control could make sure that products are made to specification.
- A technologist in middle management could serve as the communication bridge between engineering and the facility.
- In an industrial plant, a technician could remanufacture old equipment to bring it back to life.
- A technician or technologist with an interest in education could become a machine operations trainer, making sure those hospitals, companies, and individuals understand safe and effective procedures for using new equipment.

There are three choices for majoring in mechanical engineering technology or manufacturing engineering. The table below gives a basic understanding of the differences but both sections on mechanical engineering and mechanical engineering technology should be read to gain a more thorough understanding of the fields and the differences between them.

Degree Program	Degree Type	Primary Focus	Types of employers
Mechanical Engineering Technology (MET)	Associate's Degree (technician)	Installs, maintains, and repairs machines, & manufacturing systems.	Numerous companies hire ME technicians.
Mechanical Engineering Technology (MET)	Bachelor's Degree (engineering technologist)	Manage and support the design, manufacture and use of anything that moves. Plan, design, test, operate and analyze machines, processes and installations. May inspect, maintain, install or operate components, or run tests on parts and equipment in a laboratory. They may also write reports, communicate with other members on the team and give presentations about their findings..	Consulting firms; manufacturing facilities; government agencies; national laboratories; medical device companies; computer equipment companies; utility companies; and many more.
Mechanical Engineering (ME)	Bachelor's Degree (engineer)	Investigate complex mechanical problems and develop engineering methods to solve them. Manage and support the design, manufacture and use of anything that moves. Plan, design, test, operate and analyze machines, processes and installations. May inspect, maintain, install or operate components, or run tests on parts and equipment in a laboratory. They may also write reports, communicate with other members on the team and give presentations about their findings.	Consulting firms; manufacturing facilities; government agencies; national laboratories; medical device companies; computer equipment companies; utility companies; and many more.

Degree comparison table of mechanical engineering and mechanical engineering technology.

METALLURGICAL ENGINEERING
STARTING SALARY (FOR MINING ENGINEERING): $64,404
MEDIAN INCOME: $84,320

Metallurgical engineers turn raw materials into useful products. Metallurgical engineering includes processing mineral and chemical resources into metallic, ceramic or polymeric materials; creating new high strength or high performance materials; or developing new ways to refine and process materials for new consumer applications.

A strong background in the fundamentals in chemistry, mathematics and physics as well as an affinity for thermodynamics, fluids, transport phenomena, strength of materials and material properties is required.

The Department of Metallurgical and Materials Engineering at Montana Tech of the University of Montana describes the five areas of specialization in metallurgical engineering as follows:

- Mineral Processing Engineering: Mineral processing engineers take advantage of differences in physical and/ or chemical properties to develop, manage, and control processes for liberating, separating and concentrating valuable minerals in associated waste rock.

- Extractive Metallurgy: Extractive metallurgical engineers produce and purify metals from ores, concentrates and scrap using hydrometallurgical (water chemistry), electrometallurgical (electrochemistry), and/or pyrometallurgical (thermal chemistry) technologies.

- Physical Metallurgy: Physical metallurgical engineers process the metals into products by alloying, forging, rolling, casting, powdering, etc. in order to control their various chemical, physical and mechanical properties such as corrosion resistance, strength, ductility, etc.

- Materials Engineering: Materials engineers apply similar principles as the above engineers to develop the best materials for an application form, for example, ceramics, glasses and polymers as well as certain minerals and metals.

- Welding Metallurgy: Welding engineers are concerned with joining materials together, particularly metals, to produce efficient joints with minimum damage to the integrity of the materials being joined.

FEATURE ARTICLE

THE FOOTSTEPS OF A METALLURGICAL ENGINEER

Way back in the Dark Ages, when I was about 11 years old, my family used to have dinner parties – the kind with candles and good china. Being the youngest child, I was given the honor (and I really did think it was an honor) of putting out the candles after dinner. I hate that carbon black that builds up on the inside of snuffers when you put out lots of candles, so, one night when I was using Mom's pewter candle snuffer, I kept the snuffer in the flame to melt off the black stuff. Well, what do you know! The pewter snuffer melted. I then grabbed Mom's brass snuffer and tried the same experiment. I couldn't melt the brass. Why not? And there started my interest in materials. (By the way, I didn't get grounded for this science experiment, but Mom didn't leave her pewter things out anymore.)

Our neighbor at that time was the trauma surgeon for U.S. Steel in Gary, Indiana. He was able to arrange a tour of the facility for us. Do you have any idea how exciting steel mills are? The engineers sure got to do some neat stuff. It's amazing how you can take raw materials, melt them together into a liquid, and then turn it into steel plate or sheets. I still remember how amazed I was at how big those pots of molten metal were and how wild it was to see a big slab of metal get shaped into long, thin plates.

One summer my folks took us on a trip to Ontario, Canada, where we visited the Big Nickel Mine. I was fascinated by the tour guide's stories. He said the mills used to pour the slag from the molten metal down the hills and vegetation was destroyed. Then NASA used the ruined landscape to practice lunar walking. I really liked going down into the mine and learning how the ore is extracted and turned into objects we use every day.

Since we lived near Chicago we toured the Museum of Natural History and its reproduction of an actual coal mine. All these tours made me want to explore the field of materials. But, to be truthful, I didn't enter college determined to be a metallurgist. Originally, I wanted to be a chemist, but my high school chemistry teacher told me to major in engineering, instead of chemistry, so I would have a better chance of getting a good job. At Notre Dame all students take "Freshmen Studies." You don't declare a major your first year. If you think you want to be an engineer, you take physics instead of history as an elective. During freshman year I visited the metallurgical engineering department. They were very friendly and told me about the courses they offered. That's when I officially went into metallurgy.

Today, I am a systems engineer. This means that I look at the big picture for my projects. In theory, systems outranks all the other engineering disciplines. We coordinate everything to make sure that the mechanical folks don't do something to cause software too much heartburn and that operations can actually produce the gizmo. A good systems engineer has a broad knowledge of all engineering fields without necessarily being an expert in any one particular area.

Maribeth McCarthy retired from BAE SYSTEMS and now leads the Continental Math and Math Olympiad teams for Bicentennial Elementary School. She frequently demonstrates interesting material concepts for school groups.

If you are interested in a career in materials science and engineering or just want to learn more about it, visit the Materials Information Society at asminternational.org.

NAVAL ARCHITECTURE

STARTING SALARY (FOR MECHANICAL ENGINEERING): $ 58,749

MEDIAN INCOME: $88,100

Naval architects are engineers who design all kinds of watercraft, or anything that can be used as transportation on or under water. This may be a ship, boat, submarine, seaplane, icebreaker, or offshore drilling platform. The vessels may be used for commerce, recreation, or naval operations, and can be big or small. They may be powered by sails, diesel, or gas turbine engines, electricity, or nuclear power.

Marine environments are tricky. One minute the seas are calm and the next can be a white-knuckle ride as the waves pound the side of your boat or seagoing vessel. To design for this unpredictability provides a challenge for the naval architect. Naval architects design boats with the following elements in mind:

- Hydrostatics—the study of the pressures exerted on the hull. For example, buoyancy is a hydrostatic force which enables an object to float.
- Stability—the boat's ability to remain afloat and right itself after a strong wind or wave.
- Hydrodynamics—the study of water in motion around the ship. It includes powering through the water, maneuvering and controlling the direction of the vessel, as well as the effects of water resistance around the hull.
- Strength, structure and construction—the selection of materials for the hull as well as the rudder, steering, and propeller design. Naval architects analyze the ocean forces that the boat may encounter during a storm at sea. This

also includes the boat's strength in a collision or during accidental grounding.

- Interior Design. Ships are complicated, self-sufficient structures. They must carry all of the systems that enable the crew to live aboard for weeks or months at a time. Naval architects decide on the arrangement of the cabin, sleeping quarters, galley, head (bathroom), ventilation, fire protection, floor plan, capacity, water and sewage, weapons (on naval ships), propulsion, and cargo handling.

Naval architects often test the performance of newly designed boats and vessels in long towing tanks. These tanks are typically housed in government laboratories and universities around the U.S. and the world.

As you can see, naval architects have many considerations for each design element. There are some stock designs available for mass production boats, but the future of ship design is wide open. Every time a materials engineer designs a lighter, stronger, or faster hull, rudder, or propeller, it has the potential to change the hydrostatics, hydrodynamics, construction techniques, strength, or interior design of future boats and ships. Every time a  new paper is published or new research is completed, there are opportunities for advancement, changes in existing strategies, and new horizons to sail.

For more information about naval architecture and preparing to work as a naval architect, visit the Society of Naval Architects and Marine Engineers at www.sname.org or pick up a copy of *The Maritime Engineer: Careers in Naval Architecture and Marine, Ocean and Naval Engineering*.

Ocean Engineering

Median Starting Salary (for Mechanical Engineering): $ 58,749

Median Income: $84,770

Miles below the surface, a remotely operated vehicle (ROV) or underwater robot is exploring the ocean floor. The ROV may be taking pictures, collecting samples of the ocean floor, recovering treasures from a shipwreck, or actually performing repairs on an underwater structure such as an oil platform. In the tragic BP oil spill of 2010, underwater robots were the first line of defense

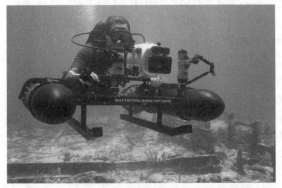

to try to repair the spewing oil pipe. Every instrument, every device and every process in an ocean environment is the creation and responsibility of ocean engineers. These engineers are at the top of their game because the ocean environment is so corrosive, volatile and often changeable. Waves are never-ending and the devices or gear that is used to explore the environment must be able to withstand the "typical" forces of mother nature such as high winds, waves and salt-water.

Ocean engineering is a fast growing and dynamic field with plentiful opportunities that are improving as people turn to the oceans for resources such as food, transportation, and energy. Ocean engineers must be creative and visionary to see their potential to use the oceans effectively. Government, industry and academia are hungry for ocean experts and researchers to develop new processes and systems to explore this natural resource with minimal or no danger to its habitat and environment.

One of the great things about ocean engineering is that many different types of engineers can be a part of the solutions needed for ocean infrastructure, research and utilization. Ocean engineering integrates disciplines such as materials science and mechanical, civil, computer, software, marine, chemical and electrical and electronics engineering. In addition to creating ROVs, they also develop underwater structures, oil rigs, buoys for data collection, and they are hard at work developing ways to capture the energy of waves and turn them into electricity. They develop transportation systems, plan new uses for waterways, design deep-water ports, and integrate the land and water transportation systems and methods. They are concerned with discovering, producing, and transporting offshore petroleum as sources of energy and developing new ways to protect marine wildlife and beaches against the unwanted consequences of offshore oil production.

Ocean engineers study all aspects of the ocean environment to determine our effect on the oceans, the ocean as a natural resource, and its effects on ships and other marine vehicles and structures.

For more information on ocean engineering be sure to read the section on petroleum engineering. Also, visit the Society of Naval Architects and Marine Engineers (SNAME) website at www.sname.org for information about their student sections and scholarship information or pick up a copy of *The Maritime Engineer: Careers in Naval Architecture and Marine, Ocean and Naval Engineering* at engineeringedu.com.

OPTICAL ENGINEERING

MEDIAN STARTING SALARY (FOR ELECTRICAL ENGINEERING): $ 57,300

MEDIAN INCOME (FOR ELECTRICAL ENGINEERING): $89,630

Optical engineering is a progressive and exciting field. Optical engineers design and develop devices and measurement systems such as lasers, telescopes, and fiber optics that use the properties of light. They figure out how to bend, bounce, guide, scatter, colorize, block, and catch light to enhance medicine, make our lives more comfortable (your TV remote control uses light to change the channel) and allow us to see objects that are too tiny or too far away for the human eye.

Lasers are used in many different kinds of applications. Medical doctors use lasers to cut out birthmarks and cancerous growths, detached retinas, cauterize wounds, and vaporize kidney stones. Your home and car CD players use laser light to play your favorite music and holograms on credit cards are made with lasers. Laser printers and supermarket scanners are other examples of how laser technology has merged into our lives.

Fiber optics is another expanding branch of optical engineering. Fiber optics are hair-sized strands of glass that carry voice and video information over long distances in the form of pulses of light. Fiber optic systems run all over the world. They run across the country and even underwater to neighboring countries.

Optical engineers may design virtual reality games or air-combat simulators. They may seek to optimize CD storage capacity or develop new medical applications such as telemedicine. They may focus on making the Internet faster and more accessible. Currently there are only five accredited optical engineering programs in the United States. For more information, visit the International Society for Optics and Photonics at www.spie.org.

PETROLEUM ENGINEERING

STARTING SALARY: $ 83,121
MEDIAN INCOME: $114,080

Petroleum engineers identify and solve problems in the oil and natural gas industries. They apply their knowledge to the exploration, exploitation, drilling, production, processing, and transportation of recovered hydrocarbons from beneath the earth's surface. They face these unique challenges by using physical, mathematical, and engineering principles to produce petroleum products as well as nuclear and synthetic fuels. The oil and gas excavation process begins with geologists, who search for geological clues of their presence. When a possible source is found, sound waves are bounced off the formations of the reservoir within the earth to determine the presence of oil or gas. Then drilling teams move in. This can mean that a new road has to be built to reach a remote part of the landscape, or an oil rig needs to be built for ocean harvesting. Once the petroleum is out of the ground, it must be transported to oil refineries or gas processing plants. Processing yields such products as jet fuel, gasoline, and asphalt. Plastic, Styrofoam™, clothing (polyester), and carpet fibers are also created from crude oil at chemical facilities.

Petroleum engineering is a multidisciplinary field that incorporates teams of specialists to maintain a high level of production. Chemical engineers work on petroleum production processes, research and development, and safety; mechanical engineers work on the mechanical applications of harvesting and refining petroleum; environmental engineers may be involved with environmental monitoring and clean-up processes; and geological engineers work closely to develop innovative drilling techniques.

For more information about petroleum engineering, check out the petroleum division of the ASME at www.asme.org or the Fuels and Petrochemicals division of the AIChE at www.fapd.aiche.org.

PHARMACEUTICAL ENGINEERING
STARTING SALARY (FOR CHEMICAL ENGINEERING): $65,403
STARTING SALARY (FOR BIOMEDICAL ENGINEERING): $68,000
MEDIAN INCOME (FOR CHEMICAL ENGINEERING): $94,350
MEDIAN INCOME (FOR BIOMEDICAL ENGINEERING): $86,960

Pharmaceutical engineering is one of the newest types of engineering. On average, a medium sized pharmaceutical company employs 400-500 engineers. The pharmaceutical engineers of the future will possess an intriguing blend of engineering, science, health care, legal, and business knowledge. They understand biology, chemistry, manufacturing processes, intellectual property, drug discovery processes, business and regulatory requirements. They are innovative, creative, and hardworking. The rising cost of developing new drugs, the rising cost of medical needs, the growing age of the population, and the complexity of having drugs approved by the FDA are all responsible for the development of this new type of engineer.

Companies that make pharmaceuticals are under pressure to produce products that will not only save lives but also make life more comfortable. We have drugs to help arthritis, allergies, headaches, body aches, stomach aches, chest pains, and almost everything else you can think of. Today, when we feel bad, we take a pill, get a shot, or rub a cream or ointment on an afflicted area. We can do this thanks to the pharmaceutical industry.

But behind the scenes, the pharmaceutical industry is complex, highly regulated, and very expensive. The cost of developing a new drug, according to the 2003 Tufts Center for the Study of Drug Development, is $900 million. The average time for a drug to make it to a bottle in your local pharmacy is seven years. For every 5000 new medications that are put through extensive development, laboratory tests and animal tests, only five will make it to human clinical trials.

The clinical trials phase of the development process is divided into three phases. Phase I, an 18-month process, consists of giving the drug to a small group (fewer than 100) of healthy volunteers to study how the drug is absorbed, how it works, and how it is excreted. Phase II, a two-year process, consists of giving the drug to people with the disease the drug was designed to help and measuring the effectiveness and side effects. In the last phase, a three and one-half year process, the drug is given to a very large group (up to 5,000 people) to monitor its long-term effects on treating the disease. During this final phase, only one out of the five drugs that advanced to the clinical trials stage will receive FDA approval.

The pharmaceutical engineer is a boon to this industry because he or she can help streamline the process from development, through trials to manufacturing. Engineers solve problems, and in this industry, reducing costs and ensuring that more drugs actually receive FDA approval is an ongoing battle. In this environment, this type of engineer works with biologists, chemists, regulators, pharmacists, and other scientists.

Other environments that employ pharmaceutical engineers are pharmaceutical production facilities. Engineers may develop laboratories, develop new ways to provide sterile environments or "clean rooms," or they may adjust the chemical balance of water that is used to create new drugs. These engineers may become involved in creating new vaccines or diagnostic equipment (similar to biomedical engineering), or they may play a role in developing new gene therapies. The available opportunities in this industry are plentiful, and the need for this engineer is growing quickly. Pharmaceutical engineers can expect a promising future that is full of challenging opportunities and lucrative rewards.

For more information visit the Society for Pharmaceutical and Medical Device Professionals (ISPE) at www.ispe.org or the Biomedical Engineering Society at www.bmes.org.

PLASTICS ENGINEERING
STARTING SALARY (FOR MATERIALS ENGINEERING): $ 62,000
MEDIAN INCOME (FOR MATERIALS ENGINEERING): $85,150

A growing branch of materials engineering that often goes unnoticed is plastics engineering. More than 1.3 million people are employed designing, manufacturing, and producing plastic. The plastics industry is the fourth largest manufacturing industry in the nation. Plastics have enhanced nearly every aspect of our lives. The safety features in our cars, medicine bottles, the insulation of electrical wires – none of these would be possible without plastics.

Plastics engineers may rearrange the molecules of materials such as wood, petroleum, coal, or natural gas to create new artificial materials. They may design new parts for automobiles, develop lighter and less intrusive artificial body parts, or invent new forms of plastic that can be substituted for paper, wood, metal, or ceramic.

According to "Talk it Up!", a series of fact sheets about the safety of plastics by the American Plastics Council and the SPE, "Plastics have played an important role in keeping us safe and improving the overall quality of our lives. As plastics engineers, you recognize the many contributions plastics make to our daily lives. For example, plastics help protect our food from bacteria and our policemen from bullets. Plastics also help amputees walk again and athletes play again. In fact, you could say that plastics help make our lives the way we want them to be."

For more information about plastics engineering and the opportunities available, visit the SPE website at www.4spe.org. The University of Massachusetts, Lowell is currently the only accredited plastics engineering program in the United States.

ROBOTIC ENGINEERING

STARTING SALARY (FOR MANUFACTURING ENGINEERING): $ 58,581

MEDIAN INCOME (FOR MECHANICAL ENGINEERING): $ 80,580

Robotic engineering is an exciting field with a wide range of newly developing applications. Because of technological leaps in the computer industry, many new opportunities will emerge for robotic engineers. Robotic engineers design and maintain robots, and research new applications for robots. Robots have enormous potential for society. Equipped with the proper sensors, robots can inspect the quality of meat, measure the pollution emissions  of manufacturing plants, assist in surgery, detect corrosion in sewer pipes, investigate the depths of a volcano, or assess the speed of a tornado. Robots can improve our standard of living and give us more information about our planet or even the solar system. Such advances can open new doors for space or sea exploration.

Robots have been used primarily in the manufacturing industry, which continues to be the primary employer of robotics engineers. Automobiles are often built with the aid of a programmable machine that incorporates great precision, speed, and power. Robotics is also expanding to mining, agriculture, and other fields that are hazardous or undesirable to people. Robotic engineers work closely with computer programmers, electrical, mechanical and manufacturing engineers, and production managers.

Robotic engineers decide how the controls of a robot will work. For example, a mechanical engineer who is working on robots will design a sensor to detect light, food, tilting, and so forth; the robotics engineer will design how the sensor will be controlled and incorporated into the robot.

There are two main types of robots:

REMOTELY OPERATED VEHICLE (ROV) - ROVs are robots that are operated with a cable or tether. They can be any shape or size, and are usually designed for the specific job they will perform. Underwater ROVs search for treasure or artifacts, research the lives of sea creatures, salvage materials on the ocean floor, and maintain oil rigs or other underwater structures. Usually, an ROV is unmanned—meaning that no man, woman, or child is riding in or on the robot.

Usually, the ROV operator has a hand-held control device, similar to a video game controller, that is used to give the robot commands and power (electricity). The advantage of this system is that the ROV does not need an on-board battery, and if a video camera is attached, the footage can be seen in real time.

AUTONOMOUS VEHICLES (AV) - Autonomous means that the robot can be operated without a tether. If you have ever seen the LEGO® Mindstorms kit or watched a robotic competition, you know what I mean. These robots swap the tether for wireless or Bluetooth communication. Similar to the ROV, they can be operated by a person using a videogame-like controller directly or by a computer that has been programmed to give it specific commands.

Robot soccer is an excellent example of the complexity involved in creating artificial intelligence. The first Robot World Cup

Initiative (RoboCup) was held in Japan in 1997 and has been an annual event ever since. Imagine a robot sensing the location of the orange soccer ball, chasing the ball, and outmaneuvering other players to eventually score a goal. The competitions usually feature teams of robots ranging in size from so small they'll compete on a ping-pong table-sized field to the size of adult humans. A key goal of the RoboCup competition is to create a team of fully autonomous soccer-playing robots that will beat the human world champion soccer team by the year 2050.

The University of Southern California (USC) competed with five "soccer-bots" that could spin and twirl on individual spherical truck wheels. The USC soccer-bots were created from modified radio-controlled toy trucks. Each robot received a Pentium-powered brain and a digital eye. The Pentium laptop was mounted onto each player's back and connected to the eye. Wei-Min Shen, the computer science professor heading the project, said, "The complexity of such a task is extraordinary. Just getting the robot to distinguish between a soccer ball and a human leg requires months of programming. Sometimes their eyes detect the red hue in flesh and mistake it for the orange in a soccer ball."

Robotic competitions have become extremely popular and are a great way to gain exposure to engineering and manufacturing. There are hundreds of robotic competitions every year all around the world. Competitions range from underwater robots to aerial robots to sumo robots to First Robotics, BEST Robotics and Battlebots. Prizes include cash, scholarships, T-shirts, and much more. More information about robotic engineering can be found at the Robotics International of the Society of Manufacturing Engineers (RI/SME) website at www.sme.org and at the IEEE Robotics and Automation Society website located at www.ieee-ras.org.

SOFTWARE ENGINEERING

MEDIAN STARTING SALARY (FOR COMPUTER ENGINEERING): $67,800

MEDIAN INCOME (FOR COMPUTER ENGINEERING): $103,980

Software engineering is on the cutting edge of technology. As the world becomes more computerized, software engineering, a very progressive field, is in high in demand. Software enables us to use computers. It is the translator between humans and computers. Without software, a computer would be nothing but ones and zeros.

Software engineers apply the principles and techniques of computer science, engineering, and mathematical analysis to the design, development, testing, evaluation, analysis, and maintenance of the software, apps, operating systems, compilers, and network distributions that enable computers to perform their many applications. In programming, or coding, software engineers instruct a computer, cell phone, and/or mobile device, line by line, how to perform a specific function. They must have strong problem solving and programming skills but may be more concerned with developing algorithms and analyzing and solving programming problems than with actually writing code. Anyone in this field must be prepared to be a life-long learner, because this field  changes quickly as companies race to market with new ideas and concepts to stay on the cutting edge.

A popular branch of software engineering is coordinating, overseeing, and developing the growth, construction, and maintenance of a company's computer system. Engineers working in this capacity will assess each department's needs and make recommendations for intranets (hardwired or Wi-Fi), telephone systems, or other inter-company communication systems. They may also configure and install new systems, and train employees on the use of them. In addition, they may be a member of technical support and become experts at ensuring security.

The current demand for software engineers far exceeds the supply. The largest employers of software engineers include familiar names, such as Apple, Microsoft, Google, eBay, Facebook, Motorola, Autodesk, Blackberry, AOL, Sony, Adobe, Symantec, and Nintendo. This list is by no means exhaustive. To find more employers, simply look at who makes the software on any computer. There are thousands of software manufacturers that hire software engineers.

To prepare for a career in software engineering, you need to gain exposure to as many programming languages as possible. Popular job requirements include C/C++, Unix, OLE, Pearl, Java, PhP, Cisco, HTML, CGI Coding, Windows, and Novell. Go to the websites of the popular software engineer employers and check out their job postings to keep current with the inevitable rapid changes this industry will witness. Some software engineers develop both packaged systems and systems software or create customized applications. Visit the website of the Software Engineering Institute at www.sei.cmu.edu.

STRUCTURAL ENGINEERING

MEDIAN STARTING SALARY (FOR CIVIL ENGINEERING): $51,793

MEDIAN INCOME (FOR CIVIL ENGINEERING): $79,340

A career in structural engineering offers numerous and diverse opportunities. Structural engineering focuses not only on the design and development of structures such as houses, coliseums,

bridges, and shopping malls but on the design and development of materials that will create these structures. The structural engineering profession offers exciting challenges and potential for growth. Each day brings new and more sophisticated materials that will change the shape and the future of structures.

Structural engineers must be creative and resourceful. They must visualize the framework of a structure and determine what forces will produce what loads upon it. Many structural engineers in California design buildings that are able to sustain ground-shaking (earthquake) loads.

Structural engineers may work as governmental building inspectors, as designers, or as construction consultants for architectural and construction firms. Some consult on building renovation or research ways to develop new and stronger materials. The challenge in structural engineering is not just designing and developing the best and safest structure, but designing and developing new ways to test, remodel, or construct structures inexpensively without compromising safety or personal integrity. For more information, visit the Structural Engineering Institute (SEI) of the ASCE website at www.seinstitute.org.

For more information about structural engineering and preparing to work as a civil/structural engineer, pick up a copy of *From Sundaes to Space Stations: Careers in Civil Engineering.*

SYSTEMS ENGINEERING

STARTING SALARY (FOR INDUSTRIAL ENGINEERING): $58,581

MEDIAN INCOME (FOR INDUSTRIAL ENGINEERING): $78,860

According to the systems engineering department at George Mason University, "Systems Engineering is the 'people-oriented engineering profession.' Systems Engineers determine the most effective ways for an organization to use all of a given system's components – people, machines, materials, information, and energy. Systems engineers plan, design, implement and manage complex systems that assure performance, safety, reliability, maintainability at reasonable cost and delivered on time."

Systems engineers take pieces or parts from several different sectors and integrate them into a complete unit or process. For example, a systems engineer working in the telecommunications industry may work with computer or software engineers to develop a program, with mechanical engineers to design the parts, and with electronic engineers to design the circuit boards for a new disposable cell phone or telephone system. Most systems have mechanical or electrical aspects and may include one or more computers as well. A systems engineer is a specialist in integrating the pieces of a system into a process or into an effective whole. For example, an automobile is an integrated system. Electrical engineers create the electrical aspects such  as the ignition and dashboard; m a t e r i a l s engineers work with the materials aspects such as designing for aerodynamics or developing puncture resistant tires; mechanical engineers deal with the mechanical aspects such as creating high performance suspensions or lubrication systems. The systems engineer is responsible for bringing all of these components together to produce a car. The challenge associated with a complex system is to foresee or handle side effects that may occur when separate parts are brought together. The dashboard or suspension may not meet the aerodynamics specifications of the materials engineer, and the tires may not meet the suspension specifications of the mechanical engineer. The individual products may need to be redesigned to work together.

Have you ever wondered how supermarkets and large stores keep their inventories of goods in balance? How they deliver those goods on time? How computers and automobiles are manufactured with quality and at competitive prices? How 1-800 and calling-card calls are handled and routed automatically through the telephone network? How thousands of airplanes and millions of travelers are scheduled and managed efficiently on a daily basis? The answer is systems engineering.

For more information, contact the control systems technical division of the society of the IEEE at www.ieeecss.org.

TELECOMMUNICATIONS ENGINEERING

MEDIAN STARTING SALARY (FOR ELECTRICAL ENGINEERING): **$57,600**

MEDIAN INCOME (FOR ELECTRICAL ENGINEERING): **$89,630**

Telecommunications is a specialization within electrical engineering that is expected to grow by leaps and bounds. Cellular telephones, palm-pilots, videophones, and wireless communication are everywhere. Satellite signals, microwaves, and fiber-optic trunks are all part of the specialized telecommunications industry.

Communications possibilities that were not dreamed of a few years ago -- video cell phones, online video conferencing, and international broadcasting of concerts, conferences and tutorials -- are transforming the telecommunication field. Teamwork between engineers, software designers, and artists is required to design the devices of tomorrow. Wireless networks are dominating the market and have become as reliable as the fiber-optic lines. Major cities such as Portland, Oregon are already delivering free wireless Internet to every home and business. Innovative

companies will rush to market with products such as wearable computers and components that combine micro-technologies into miniature chip sets. Specialized network equipment for new and innovative applications will become available, and existing network equipment will be upgraded or replaced. Exciting new technologies will create new jobs; the opportunities are only limited by your imagination.

Major communications service providers in the United States that employ telecommunications engineers include AT&T, Bell Companies (Bell-South, Pacific Bell, etc.), Comcast, GTE,

Verizon, NTT, Sprint, and TCI. Other large employers, such as Bellcore, Cisco, Ericsson, Lucent Technologies (including Bell Laboratories), Newbridge, Nokia, and Nortel, focus on research and product development. For more information, visit the IEEE website at www.ieee.org.

TRANSPORTATION ENGINEERING

MEDIAN STARTING SALARY (FOR CIVIL ENGINEERS): $51,793
MEDIAN INCOME (FOR CIVIL ENGINEERS): $79,340

Transportation engineering is a branch of civil engineering whose goal is to allow people and goods to move safely, rapidly, conveniently, and efficiently. Transportation engineers design streets, highways, and public transportation systems. They design parking lots and traffic flow patterns that will prevent major congestion at busy intersections, shopping malls, and sporting events. They are involved in planning and designing airports, railroads, and busy pedestrian thoroughfares.

According to the Institute of Transportation Engineers  (ITE), the field of transportation engineering became essential because "the rapid development of automotive transportation following the First World War and the resultant accidents and congestion in the early 20's were responsible for public demands that expert attention be directed to the alleviation of traffic ills." During this period, engineers largely concentrated their work in the field of traffic regulatory devices and roadway design and re-design. Today, as you observe the 5:00 PM traffic in any major city, you can see that transportation engineering plays an even larger and more necessary part of our society.

Transportation engineering is an exciting field that will see increased demand over the next ten years. Whether you like to work indoors or outdoors, transportation engineering has something for you. For example, you can create computer models of new shopping centers and universities or work outside solving on-site construction problems. According to Reed Brockman, author of *From Sundaes to Space Stations: Careers in Civil Engineering*, "when you think of being a transportation engineer, think of yourself as part sculptor, part lawyer and part environmentalist."

Imagine being called as an expert witness in a court of law because you designed a specific transportation system. Many transportation engineers work as private consultants or in research. Federal, state, and local agencies also employ an abundance of transportation engineers.

The (ITE) has an informative website at www.ite.org. For more information about transportation engineering and preparing to work as a civil/transportation engineer, pick up a copy of *From Sundaes to Space Stations: Careers in Civil Engineering.*

Appendix
50 Reasons to Become an Engineer

1. 48 countries (2.8 billion people) could face fresh water shortages by 2025.
2. Population in developed countries will age and engineers can help develop assistive technologies so aging people can maintain healthy, productive lifestyles.
3. To improve the quality of the air we breathe.
4. To improve the quality of the water we drink.
5. To improve the quality of the food we eat.
6. To save the rainforests.
7. To save rare or exotic animals from extinction.
8. To improve battery technology for electric cars.
9. To conserve our natural resources by improving recycling systems and methods.
10. To educate a potential President of the United States.
11. To help the energy crisis by finding new ways to produce or store solar, wind, wave, geothermal and other sources of alternative energy.
12. To find ways to make nuclear waste non-toxic.
13. To develop safe nuclear energy.
14. To help find a cure for AIDS.
15. To help develop new medicines for numerous diseases.
16. To invent smaller, more affordable computers.
17. To make better theme parks and safer roller coasters.
18. To keep up with the technology needs of society.
19. So the U.S. won't lose its power to other countries.
20. To educate the next generation.
21. To reverse engineer the brain.
22. To counter the violence of terrorists.
23. To improve methods of instruction and learning.
24. To create better virtual reality systems.
25. To capture carbon dioxide.
26. To sustain the infrastructure of cities and living spaces.
27. To explore other galaxies.
28. To understand more about our planet.

29. To reduce our vulnerability to assaults in cyberspace.
30. To prevent devastation from hurricanes and other natural disasters.
31. To improve transportation on land, sea and air.
32. To improve our connectivity and ability to communicate with family and friends.
33. To help us save money on everything.
34. To keep us safe at home and in other countries.
35. To lessen our vulnerability to disease.
36. To keep our oceans clean.
37. To explore the depths of the ocean.
38. To help our pets live longer.
39. To aid veterinarians in caring for animals.
40. To minimize our footprint on the Earth.
41. To prevent car accidents with better traffic infrastructure.
42. To create green buildings that can power themselves.
43. To understand the oceans and their ability to help us.
44. To reduce the impact of war.
45. To lessen the need for war.
46. To enhance the beauty of our surroundings.
47. To have better furniture and computer peripherals that reduce our risk of carpal tunnel or back pain.
48. To save the polar bears and other endangered species.
49. To get more people where they need to go quickly, safely and conveniently.
50. To decrease the incidence of disease and famine.

ABET Accredited Programs in Engineering

There are 39 programs in engineering
1. Aerospace Engineering
2. Agricultural Engineering
3. Architectural Engineering
4. Automotive Engineering
5. Bioengineering
6. Biomedical Engineering
7. Biological Engineering
8. Ceramic Engineering
9. Chemical Engineering
10. Civil Engineering
11. Computer Engineering
12. Construction Engineering
13. Electrical/Electronics Engineering
14. Electromechanical Engineering
15. Engineering Management
16. Engineering Mechanics
17. Engineering Physics
18. Engineering Science
19. Environmental Engineering
20. Fire Protection Engineering
21. Forest Engineering
22. General Engineering
23. Geological Engineering
24. Industrial Engineering
25. Manufacturing Engineering
26. Materials Engineering
27. Mechanical Engineering
28. Metallurgical Engineering
29. Mining Engineering
30. Naval Architecture and Marine Engineering
31. Nuclear and Radiological Engineering
32. Ocean Engineering
33. Optics Engineering
34. Petroleum Engineering
35. Photonics Engineering
36. Software Engineering
37. Systems Engineering
38. Telecommunications Engineering
39. Welding Engineering

ABET Accredited Programs in Engineering Technology

There are 29 accredited programs in engineering technology
1. Aeronautical Engineering Technology
2. Aerospace Engineering Technology
3. Air Conditioning Engineering Technology
4. Architectural Engineering Technology
5. Automotive Engineering Technology
6. Biomedical Engineering Technology
7. Chemical Engineering Technology
8. Civil Engineering Technology
9. Computer Engineering Technology
10. Construction Engineering Technology
11. Electrical/Electronics Engineering Technology
12. Electromechanical Engineering Technology
13. General Engineering Technology
14. Environmental Engineering Technology
15. Fire Protection Engineering Technology
16. Industrial Engineering Technology
17. Information Engineering Technology
18. Instrumentation and Control Systems Engineering Technology
19. Manufacturing Engineering Technology
20. Mechanical Engineering Technology
21. Mining Engineering Technology
22. Naval Architecture and Marine Engineering Technology
23. Nuclear and Radiological Engineering Technology
24. Optics Engineering Technology
25. Petroleum Engineering Technology
26. Photonics Engineering Technology
27. Surveying and Geomatics Engineering Technology
28. Telecommunications Engineering Technology
29. Welding Engineering Technology

Bibliography/ Recommended Reading

AAUW: "Gender Gaps: Where Schools Still Fail Our Children," Washington, DC, 1998.

Astin, Alexander. What Matters in College?: Four Critical Years Revisited. San Francisco: Jossey-Bass, 1997.

Basta, Nicholas. Opportunities in Engineering Careers. Chicago: VGM Career Horizons, 1990.

Baine, Celeste. Engineers Make a Difference: Motivating Student to Pursue an Engineering Education. Eugene, OR: Bonamy Publishing, 2008.

———. "The Green Engineer: Engineering Careers to Save the Earth." Eugene, OR: Bonamy Publishing, 2011.

———. "Ideas in Action. A Girl's Guide to Careers in Engineering." Eugene, OR: Bonamy Publishing, 2009.

———. "The Musical Engineer: A Music Enthusiast's Guide to Careers in Music Engineering and Technology." Eugene, OR: Bonamy Publishing, 2007.

———. "The Maritime Engineer: Careers in Naval Architecture and Marine, Ocean and Naval Engineering." Eugene, OR: Bonamy Publishing, 2010.

———. "The Fantastical Engineer: A Thrillseeker's Guide to Careers in Theme Park Engineering." Second Ed. Eugene, OR: Bonamy Publishing, 2007.

———. "High Tech Hot Shots: Careers in Sports Engineering." Alexandria, VA: National Society of Professional Engineers, 2004.

Bolles, Richard Nelson. "What Color is your Parachute?: A Practical Manual for Job Hunters and Career Changers." Berkeley: Ten Speed Press, 2001.

Brockman, Reed. "From Sundaes to Space Stations: Careers in Civil Engineering." Eugene, OR: Bonamy Publishing, 2010.

"Careers in Science and Engineering: A Student Guide to Grad School and Beyond." National Academy Press, 1996.

Carnegie, Dale. How to Win Friends and Influence People. New York: Simon & Schuster, 1994.

Catsambis, S. "The Path to Math: Gender and Racial-Ethnic Differences in Mathematics Participation From Middle to High School," Sociology of Education 67 (1994): pp. 199-215.

Congressional Commission on the Advancement of Women and Minorities in Science Engineering and Technology Development, "Land of Plenty," Arlington, VA, Sept. 2000.

Etzkowitz, Henry, Carol Kemelgor, and Michael Neuschatz. "Barriers to Women in Academic Science and Engineering." Baltimore: John Hopkins University Press, 1994.

Ferguson, Eugene S. Engineering and the Mind's Eye. Cambridge: MIT Press, 1997.

Ferrell, Tom. "Peterson's Job Opportunities for Engineering and Computer Science Majors." United States: Thomson Learning, 1999.

Florman, Samual C. The Introspective Engineer. New York: St. Martin's Press, 1996.

Gabelman, Irving. "The New Engineer's Guide to Career Growth and Professional Awareness." New York: IEEE Press, 1996.

"The Green Report: Engineering Education for a Changing World." American Society for Engineering Education, 1998.

Kelnhofer, Richard, Robert Stangeway, Edward Chandler, & Owe Peterson. 2010. "Future of Engineering Technology." In Proceedings of the 2010 ASEE Annual Conference & Exposition, Session 1648, Louisville, Kentucky, June 20-23.

Land, Ronald E. "Engineering Technologists are Engineers." Journal of Engineering Technology, Spring 2012,Vol 29, no. 1.

Landis, Raymond B. "Studying Engineering: A Roadmap to a Rewarding Career." Burbank, CA: Discovery Press, 1995.

———. "Enhancing Student Success: A Five Step Process for Getting Students to 'Study Smart'." American Society for Engineering Education, Washington, DC, 1998.

———. "Enhancing Engineering Student Success: A Pedagogy for Changing Behaviors." American Society for Engineering Education, Washington, DC, 1997.

LeBold, William K. and Dona J. LeBold. "Women Engineers: A Historical Perspective." American Society for Engineering Education, Washington, DC, 1998.

Love, Sydney F. Planning and Creating Successful Engineered Designs: Managing the Design Process. Los Angeles: Advanced Professional Development Incorporated, 1986.

Morgan, Robert P. Proctor P. Reid, and Wm, A. Wulf, "The Changing Nature of Engineering." ASEE PRISM, May-June 1998.

The National Science Foundation. "Women, Minorities and Persons with Disabilities in Science and Engineering: 2000." Washington, DC, Sept. 2000.

Peters, Robert L. Getting What You Came For: The Smart Student's Guide to Earning a Master's or Ph.D. New York: Farrar, Straus and Giroux, 1997.

Peterson, George D. "Engineering Criteria 2000: A Bold New Change Agent." American Society for Engineering Education, Washington, DC, 1998.

Petroski, Henry. "Invention by Design: How Engineers Get from Thought to Thing." Cambridge: Harvard University Press, 1996.

————. To Engineer is Human: The Role of Failure in Successful Design. New York: Vintage Books, 1992.

————. The Evolution of Useful Things: How Everyday Artifacts-From Forks and Pins to Paper Clips and Zippers-Came to be as They Are. New York: Vintage Books, 1992.

"Planning a Career in Biomedical Engineering." Biomedical Engineering Society, Baltimore, 1996.

Sherwood, Kaitlin. "Women in the Engineering Industry." Society of Women Engineers at UIUC lecture, 1994.

"Simple Machines." Society of Women Engineers Career Guidance Module, Chicago, 1996.

"Student Science Training Programs for Precollege Students." Science Service, Inc., New York, 1994.

Taylor, K.D.; Buchanan, W.W.; Englund, R.B.; O'Connor, T.P.; Yates, D.W.; , "Professional registration issues for engineering technology graduates: a range of perspectives," Frontiers in Education Conference, 1997. 27th Annual Conference. Teaching and Learning in an Era of Change. Proceedings. , vol.2, no., pp.1006-1010 vol.2, 5-8 Nov 1997

Tieger, Paul and Barbara Barron-Tieger. Do What You Are: Discover the Perfect Career for You through the Secrets of Personality Type. Boston: Little, Brown and Company, 1995.

Tietsen, Jill S. and Kristy A Schloss with Carter, Bishop, and Kravits. Keys to Engineering Success. New Jersey: Prentice Hall, 2001.

U.S. Labor Statistics: JOBS 2010.

Vanderheiden, Gregg. "Thirty Something (Million): Should There Be Exceptions?" Trace Research and Development Center, Waisman Center and Department of Industrial Engineering, University of Wisconsin-Madison, 1996.

"Women, Minorities, and Persons with Disabilities in Science and Engineering: 1996," The National Science Foundation, Washington, DC, 1996.

Yantzi, Lindsay. "The Construction Industry's Orthopedic Specialist." University of Kansas-Lawrence, 1997.

Index

Symbols

2+2 Programs 51

A

ABET 20,45,46,49,50,56,85,193,194
Academic preparation 29
Academics 55
Accelerated Programs 56
ACT score 29
admission 29
Advanced Placement (AP) 29,51
advisor 53
aeronautical 42,87
Aeronautical Engineering 87-92
Aeronautical Engineering Technology 194
aerospace 87
Aerospace Engineering 87-92,193
Aerospace Engineering Technology 194
Africa 133
African Americans 65
agricultural 62
Agricultural and Biological Engineering (A&BE) 63,92-96
Agricultural Engineering 193
agricultural systems 93
AIDS 191
Air Conditioning Engineering Technology 194
Air Force 55
airplanes 22,87
air pollution 93,113,131
air conditioning 141
algebra 29
alternative energy 113,129
alternative fuel vehicles 97
American Institute of Chemical Engineers (AIChE) 7,19,112,141.164,177
American Society for Engineering Education (ASEE) 63,66
American Society of Agricultural and Biological Engineers 95
American Society of Civil Engineers (ASCE) 31,113,116,164,186

American Society of Mechanical Engineers (ASME) 7,31,42,58,84,88,164,166,177
American Academy of Environmental Engineers (AAEE) 134
American Society of Heating, Refrigerating and Air 143
amusement parks 62,71
Anderson, Mary 61
animals 77-78,192
antibiotics 139
AOL 178
Apple Computers 22,184
architects 64
architectural 42,63,78
architectural engineer 18,96
Architectural Engineering 96-97,193
Architectural Engineering Institute (AEI) 97
Architectural Engineering Technology 194
architectural firms 116
Arkwright, Richard 82
Armed Forces 55
Army 55
articulation agreements 49,51
Asian American 66
Assistive technology 104
Astin, Alexander 52
attorney 26
audio 74
Autodesk 184
automotive 42
Automotive Engineering 97-99,193
Automotive Engineering Technology 194
automotive engineers 97
Autonomous Vehicles (AV) 182

B

Bachelor of Arts (BA) in Engineering 84
back pain 192
BAE SYSTEMS 171
baseball bats 161
beauty 192
Be creative 64

BEST 30
bicycle 24
Biochemical Engineering 102
Bioelectrical Engineering 102
Bioengineering 193
biological 62
Biological Engineering 193
biological systems 93
biology 29
Biomechanical Engineering 103
biomedical 62,63,78
biomedical engineer 18,74
Biomedical Engineering 100-105,193
Biomedical Engineering Society (BMES)
    104,105,179
Biomedical Engineering Technology
    105-108,194
bioresources 93
Blackberry 184
Boeing 144
brain 191
bridge 25
Brockman, Reed 115
Brown and Caldwell 133
building design 161
buoyancy 171
Bureau of Labor Statistics 85
business 78
business plans 78

C

cabin 167
calculus 29
capacity 172
Career and Technical Education (CTE)
    51
career counselor 53
cargo handling 172
carpal tunnel 192
Carter, Jimmy 27,82
Carver, George Washington 47
cell phone companies 74
Cellular and Tissue Engineering 104
cell phone 36
Ceramic 108
Ceramic Engineering 108-110,193
Change the world 64
chemical 42,62,63,74,78
chemical engineer 18
Chemical Engineering 110-112,193
Chemical Engineering Technology 194
chemistry 29

civil 42,62,63,78
Civil Engineering 112-116,193
Civil Engineering Technology 116-
    118,194
Class sizes 49
Clean Air Act 132
clean drinking water 113
Clemson University 133
Clinical Engineering 103
CNC programmers 141
Coast Guard 55,156
collision 172
communicate 62
community college 28
computer 42,62
Computer-Aided Design and Drafting
    (CADD) 43
Computer-Aided Design (CAD) 43
Computer Engineering 119-121,193
Computer engineering technologists 121
Computer Engineering Technology 121-
    123,194
computer engineers 74
computers 191
Concrete Canoe 31
construction 42,172
construction engineer 114
Construction Engineering 193
construction engineering technologists
    116
Construction Engineering Technology
    116-118,194
Construction Management 97
contest 31
control systems 187
co-op experience 57
coal mine 172
coffee 141
communication skills 20,28
competitions 30
computer applications 29
computer programming 29
Cooperative education 57
Cost 54
creative 23
creative ideas 79
cruise lines 154
cutting and welding equipment 154
cyberspace 192

D

damage-control team 154

design engineer 18
diesel 171
diesel engines 152
digital instruments 74
digital music 22
disease 192
Disney 25,144
Disneyland 71
Disney, Walt 72
Disney World 71
diverse engineering workforce 65
doctor 26,64
Dunbar, Dr. Bonnie J. 62
Dyson 23

E

Early College high schools 51
Earth 192
eBay 22,184
effective communicators 32
electrical 62,63,74
electrical and electronic 42
Electrical and lighting systems 97
Electrical/Electronics Engineering
    Technology 128-130,194
electrical engineer 18,124
Electrical Engineering 124-127,156
electrical systems 152
electric cars 22,97
electric engines 152
electricity 171
Electromechanical Engineering 193
Electromechanical Engineering
    Technology 194
Electronic engineering technologists 128
electronics 152
electronic talking devices 104
electromechanical 42,124
emergency team 154
energy 63
engine 147
engineering firms 47
Engineering Management 193
Engineering Mechanics 193
Engineering Physics 193
Engineering Projects In Community
    Service (EPICS) 31
Engineering Science 193
engineering societies 30
engineering technician 36
engineering technologist 36
engineering technology 35

Engineer Intern (EI) 45
Engineer in Training 45
engineer's toolbox. 20
Engineers Without Borders (EWB) 70
Engineer Your Life 63
Enjoy job flexibility 64
enrollment 49
entrepreneur 26,64
Entrepreneurship 57
environmental 62,63,78
environmental engineer 113
Environmental Engineering 69,131-
    134,193
Environmental Engineering Technology
    194
EPA 132
Extractive Metallurgy 169
extracurricular activities 28
Extrovert 32

F

Facebook 22,184
Faculty 55
farm equipmen 96
Federal government 129
Femenia, Jose 147
fire protection 172
Fire Protection Engineering 135-136,193
Fire Protection Engineering Technology
    137-138,194
FIRST Robotics 30
fishing boats 152
Fitch, John 82
Fleming, Nancy 29
floor plan 172
food 93,96
Food Engineering 138
food processing 138
footwear engineer 28
Ford Motor Company 98,148
foreign oil 63
forensic engineer 18
Forest Engineering 193
fuel efficiency 97
Fundamentals of Engineering (FE) 45
furniture 192
Future City 30

G

galaxy 22
galley 172

game 79
Garland, Milton 142
gas turbines 147,166
General Engineering Technology 194
genetic 62,104
genetic engineering 137
Geological Engineering 193
Georgia Tech 82
geotechnical engineer 114
geothermal heat pumps 113
gizmo 79
golf ball 88
Google 178
Green Energy Engineering 75

H

habitats for zoos 62
Handler, Ruth 62
hands-on 48
hand tools 154
hard working 32
Hawaii 95
hazardous materials 25
HD video 22
headphones 74
healthy planet 17
hearing aids 104
helicopters 87
Henry, Beulah Louise 61
Herbert Hoover 27
higher speed 160
high-speed trains 22
Hispanic Americans 65
hockey 139
Honda 98
Honors 29
Hoover, Herbert 81
Hopper, Grace Murray 61
hull 172
hunger 92
hurricanes 192
hybrids 97
hydraulics 153
hydraulic systems 153
hydrodynamics 172,173
hydropower facilities 113
hydrostatics 172,173

I

icebreaker 172
ice cream 136
I did that 17

Imagineers 71
industrial 42,63
Industrial Engineering 143-144.193
Industrial Engineering Technology 145-
        146,194
Industrial engineers 74,140
Information Engineering Technology 194
infrastructure 191,192
ingenuity 19
Institute of Electrical and Electronic
        Engineering (IEEE)
        31,120,121,124,125,183,187,189
Institute of Industrial Engineers (IIE)
        144
Instrumentation and Control Systems
        Engineering Technology 194
Intel 22,146
Intel International Science and
        Engineering Fair (ISEF). 30
interests 33
Interior Design 172
International Bridge Building Contest 30
internships 57.See Cooperative
        education
introvert 32
inventors 22,79
inventor's log 80
iPhones 22
iPods 74
iRobot 23
irrigation 113
iTunes 74

J

job shadow 47
Jones, Amanda Theodosia 60
junior college 47

K

Kevlar 61
Knack, Susan 59
Knight, Heather 60
Kwoleks, Stephanie 61

L

Lady Edison 61
Lamarr, Hedy 61
law 56
leadership 29
LEGO Mindstorms 182
Lehr, Donald 102

Lenard, Jeff 19
liberal arts 84
licenses 153
life support engineers 78
lifetime learners 32
lighting 154
Location 54
looms 59
Lovelace, Ada Byron 60
Love your work 63
lunar walking 171

M

machine tools 154
Make a big salary 64
Make a Difference 64
management 63
manufacturing 42,63
manufacturing companies 116
manufacturing engineer 74,147
Manufacturing Engineering 147-148,193
Manufacturing engineering technologists 143
Manufacturing Engineering Technology 148-152,194
marine 42
Marine Engineering 152-155,193
Marine Engineering Technology 156-157
Marines 55
marine surveyors 155
Mars 23
mass production boats 173
Master's Degrees 41
Materials 63
Materials Engineering 158-164,169,179,193
Materials Information Society 171
materials or textile engineers 74
math 20,21
Mathcounts 30
MBA 56
McCarthy, Maribeth 171
mechanical 42,62,63,78
mechanical control systems 148
mechanical engineer 74,141,158
Mechanical Engineering 97,164-166,193
Mechanical engineering technologists 160
Mechanical Engineering Technology 166-168,194
Mechanical Systems 96
medical device companies 105
medical school 105

medicine 56
mental agility 27
mentor 53
Merchant Marines 55
Metallurgical 63
Metallurgical Engineering 169-171,193
microphones 74
Microsoft 144,184
military aircraft 87
mining 42
Mining Engineering 169-171,193
Mining Engineering Technology 194
Minorities in Engineering 65
Mississippi State 90
Mohr, Dr. Catherine 60
money 192
Montana Tech 169
Moran, Dr. Angela 60
Morrissey, Ellen 102
Motorola 184
mountain bikes 164
multimeters 129
Music 74
Music Engineering 74
music engineering technology 75
Myers-Briggs Type Indicator 32

N

NASA 77
National Center for Manufacturing Education (NCME) 150
National Guard 55
National Society of Black Engineers (NSBE) 66
National Student Clearinghouse Research Center 48
natural resources engineering 93
Naval architects 152,172
Naval Architecture 172-173,193
Naval Architecture and Marine Engineering Technology 194
Navy 55,61
NCEES Model Law 46
Never be bored 64
Nike 103,145
Nintendo 178
Northwest Invention Center 81
Notre Dame 171
nuclear 42,191
Nuclear and Radiological Engineering 193
Nuclear and Radiological Engineering Technology 194

nuclear power 172
nuclear reactors 151

O

Ocean engineering 174-175,193
ocean forces 172
oceans 192
Ocif, Jennifer 28
offshore drilling platform 172
Optical Engineering 175-176
optics 124
Optics Engineering 193
Optics Engineering Technology 194
organizational skills 29
organ transplants 139
oscilloscopes 129

P

patent 80
Peace Corps 69,133
Pennington, Mary Engle 61
Personal happiness 25
personality 32
pesticides 96
Petroleum Engineering 176-177,193
Petroleum Engineering Technology 194
pets 192
pharmaceutical 62
pharmaceutical engineer 18
Pharmaceutical Engineering 177-179
Photonics Engineering 193
Photonics Engineering Technology 194
Physical Metallurgy 169
physics 29
piezoelectric devices 160
Pixar Animation Studios 57
Plastics Engineering 179-180
Policies and Practices 45
population 59
Poster Contest 31
president of the United States 22
Priestley, Joseph 82
Principles and Practices of Engineering 45
Problem-solving 24
professional engineering license 84
Professional Engineer (PE) 45,117,155
Project Lead the Way (PLTW) 51
propeller 147,172,173
propulsion 173
pumps 153

Purdue University 31

Q

R

recycling 132
Reebok 28
refrigeration 138,153
Rehabilitation Engineering 104
Remotely Operated Vehicle (ROV) 174,181
renewable energy 93
research labs 105
Resources Magazine 95
Ride, Dr. Sally 77
Robotic Engineering 180-183
robotics 28
Robot World Cup 182
rockets 87
roller coaster 24,71,72,114,144,164,191
rudder 172,173

S

sails 172
Sanders, Ivar 126
San Jose State University 158
SAT 29
satellites 87
satellite TV 22
Saulnier, Daniel 70
School Size 55
Science 30
Scrubbing Bubbles 23
seaplane 172
sewage 173
shipyard 154
shock absorber 160
Simpson Gumpertz & Heger 59
simulation software 47
skis 161
sleeping quarters 173
smart clothes 161
smart engineer 160
Smart Engineering 159
    Airplanes
    Artificial Muscles
    Auto Industry
    Helicopter Blades
    Sound Industry
    Space Structures
    Submarines

smart people 26
smoother riding 160
snowboard 161
Sobey, Ed 81
Society of Automotive Engineers (SAE International) 99
Society of Hispanic Professional Engineers (SHPE) 67
Society of Manufacturing Engineers (SME) 31,146
Society of Naval Architects and Marine Engineers (SNAME) 154,155,173,175
software 62
Software Engineering 183-185,193
solar panels 113
solve crimes 62
Sony 184
sound barrier 22
Soviet Union 35
spacecraft 87
Space Engineering 76
space exploration 145
Space Mountain 72
space shuttle 36,87,139
speakers 74
spectrum analyzers 129
sporting goods 160
Sports engineering 73
sports science 87
Sputnik 35
stability 154,172
state university 47
steam turbines 147
steering 147,172
strength 33,172,173
strengths and weaknesses 33
stress cracks 25
structural 62
structural damage 162
structural engineer 114
Structural Engineering 96,185-186
Structural Engineering Institute (SEI) 179
structure 166

submarine 172
summer camp 27,29,33
Surveying and Geomatics Engineering Technology 194
sustainable 63
Symantec 184
Systems Engineering 186-187,193

T

Tanaka, David 57
team 28
technical college 47
Telecommunications Engineering 188,193
Telecommunications Engineering Technology 194
terrorists 191
test engineer 18
theme park 191
thermodynamics 156
third assistant engineer's license 155
Thurman, Bob 88
time-management 52
titanium knee and hip replacements. 22
tour 47
towing tanks 173
toy 79
Toyota 99
Transfer Admission Guarantee (TAG) 51
transmission 153
transportation 192
transportation engineer 114
Transportation Engineering 189-190
travel 64,87
trigonometry 29
tugboat 154
Tuition 49
TV dinner 139

U

United States Merchant Marine Academy 153
university 28
University of Massachusetts, Lowell 180
University of Montana 169
University of Southern California (USC) 182
unlicensed crew 154
underwater robots 22
University of Wyoming 139
U.S. Coast Guard 155

U.S. Department of Labor 85,97
U.S. Naval Academy 82
US Steel 170
utility companies 116,129

V

vacuum cleaner. 23
ventilation 173
venture capitalists 78
veterinarians 192
vibrate 154
vibration 160
video game companies 74
vocational school 47

W

Wang, Jaw Kai 94
war 192
Washington, George 27,81,82
wastewater treatment plants 116
water skis 161
water tanks 133
Watt, James 82
weapons 167
weaving 59
Webb Institute 154
Welding Engineering 193
Welding Engineering Technology 194
Welding Metallurgy 170
wheelchairs 104
Wichita State University 29
Wilson Sporting Goods 88
wind farms 22
wind turbines 113
Women in Engineering 59
Worcester Polytechnic Institute 142
Work with great people 64
World Health Organization 131
Wright, Charles 133
Wright brothers 87

X

Y

yacht 154

Z

zoos 62,78

Engineering Careers App

Includes:

- **40 Engineering and Technology Descriptions**
- **40 Videos About the Types of Engineering**
- **Salary Information**
- **Job Outlook for Each Discipline**
- **College Directory**
- **Scholarships**

Figure out what kind of engineer you want to be!

Only for iPhone. Available at iTunes

ABOUT THE AUTHOR

Celeste Baine, a graduate of Louisiana Tech University, is a biomedical engineer, Director of the Engineering Education Service Center and the award-winning author of over twenty books and booklets on engineering careers and education. She won the Norm Augustine Award from the National Academy of Engineering (The Norm Augustine award is given to an engineer who has demonstrated the capacity for communicating the excitement and wonder of engineering). She also won the American Society for Engineering Education's Engineering Dean Council's Award for the Promotion of Engineering Education and Careers, and is listed on the National Engineers Week website as one of 50 engineers you should meet. The National Academy of Engineering has included Celeste in their Gallery of Women Engineers and she has been named one of the Nifty-Fifty individuals who have made a major impact on the field of engineering by the USA Science and Engineering Festival. She has spent the past decade advising students and parents on the challenges and benefits of obtaining an engineering degree.